BRIDGES

TO ENGLISH 4

Protase E. Woodford
Doris Kernan

McGraw-Hill

New York   St. Louis   San Francisco   Auckland   Bogotá   Guatèmala
Hamburg   Johannesburg   Lisbon   London   Madrid   Mexico   Montreal
New Delhi   Panama   Paris   San Juan   São Paulo   Singapore   Sydney
Tokyo   Toronto

Credits

Editorial Development: Jacqueline Rebisz
Design: Catherine Gallagher
Copy Editing: Suzanne Shetler
Production: Robert Pedersen
Illustrations: Carlos Byron
Photo Research: Alan Forman

Photo Credits

The authors are indebted to the following persons and organizations for permission to include the following photographs: Pages 2, 8–9: U.S. Department of Agriculture; 5, 13, 14: New York State Department of Commerce; 22, 26–27, 28, 32–33, 36–37, 42, 44, 47, 108, 115, 116–117, 120; A.T.&T. Co.; 50, 54–55, 58–59, 130–131, 143: Lawrence Frank; 61: New York Public Library; 70: Frank Siteman/Taurus Photos; 78: Eastern Airlines; 81: Laimute E. Druskis/Taurus Photos; 88, 94: Chicago Convention & Tourism Bureau, Inc.; 91: Eric Kroll/Taurus Photos; 97: U.S. Department of Housing and Urban Development; 99: Masonite Corporation; 113: New York University Creative Services; 126, 138: S. Zeibers/Taurus Photos; 134: NBC. The cover photograph is from Woodfin Camp & Associates.

Library of Congress Cataloging in Publication Data   (Revised)

Woodford, Protase E
  Bridges to English.

  Includes index.
  1. English language—Text-books for foreigners.
I. Kernan, Doris, joint author.   II. Title.
PE1128.W758   428.2′4   80-21012
ISBN 0-07-034499-X

1 2 3 4 5 6 7 8 9 DODO 8 9 8 7 6 5 4 3 2 1

PREFACE

Bridges to English is a fully articulated series of six English language learning texts designed for the adult student whose first language is other than English. Educational, business, and professional demands, as well as cultural interests, continually force today's adult beyond national boundaries only to find that a sound working knowledge of English is indispensable. To this learner *Bridges to English* is directed.

The principal goal of the study of English is to be able to understand spoken and written English and to make oneself understood. *Bridges to English* is designed to ensure rapid acquisition of the listening, speaking, reading and writing skills necessary for effective communication. The introduction of language constructions, vocabulary, and pronunciation is carefully sequenced and controlled in order to promote efficient patterns of learning through constant reinforcement and extension of skills.

Each lesson integrates development of the listening, speaking, reading and writing skills. The lessons are organized according to the following plan:

New Words   The lesson begins with the new words which are presented in the context of sentences. Sometimes the new words are defined using vocabulary already learned. The questions and brief drills that immediately follow provide the practice which helps to make the new words an active part of the student's vocabulary.

Structure   The structure concepts of each lesson are presented by means of pattern drills. Through a varied series of oral exercises, the student has ample opportunity to learn the grammatical generalizations. A summary of each new structure item follows the oral exercises. After the summary, writing practice which focuses on the new structure concept is provided.

Verb Practice   These brief oral drills give students practice in verb functions that can be problematic for non-native speakers: two-word verbs, verbs similar in meaning, and verbs that take a variety of prepositions.

Conversation   The conversation, which appears in every other lesson, contains previously learned vocabulary and structure. It is designed to be learned with a minimum of effort. The conversation is based on a familiar situation so that the student can immediately talk about the particular situation. Unfamiliar structures are avoided. The questions which follow each conversation serve to check comprehension and permit the learner to use the vocabulary and structures of the conversation. The personal questions encourage the students to apply the situation of the conversation to their own lives.

Reading   The reading selection in each lesson allows the student to apply the newly acquired vocabulary and structure skills. It also serves to review and reinforce language skills learned in preceding lessons. A list of questions follows each reading selection, encouraging the student to discuss the material which has been read.

Lesson Review   Each new language concept is represented in the lesson review. The student is provided a variety of written practice drills in order to promote mastery of the vocabulary and structure items presented in the lesson.

Oral Review   The focus of the oral review is an illustration at the conclusion of each lesson. It serves as a stimulus for oral and written expression, requiring the utilization of the material presented in the lesson.

ABOUT THE AUTHORS

Protase E. Woodford is Associate Director, International Office, Educational Testing Service, Princeton, New Jersey. Formerly he was Director of Language Programs at ETS with responsibility for many language tests, including the TOEFL. He has had extensive language teaching experience at the secondary and college levels and has taught methods at the University of Texas. He has developed an English testing program sponsored by the government of Japan for Japanese business personnel. He has worked extensively with Latin American ministries of education in the area of tests and measurements. He has also worked with the British Council and the English-Speaking Union in developing common descriptors of English language ability. Mr. Woodford has given numerous speeches on language teaching methodology in Europe, Asia, Latin America, Canada, and the United States. He is the author of several language textbooks.

Doris Kernan is presently a Learning Consultant for the South Orange/ Maplewood, New Jersey, Public Schools. Ms. Kernan has taught at all levels of instruction from the elementary to the college level. She has lectured on language teaching methodology and learning psychology in the United States, Europe, Canada, Central America, and Africa. Ms. Kernan is the author of several books for the teaching of English.

CONTENTS _____

BRIDGES

TO ENGLISH 4

LESSON 1

NEW WORDS

1   Mrs. Jones lives on a farm.
    She is feeding the horse.
    She fed it yesterday, too.
    The other animals are hungry,
       too.
    They are making a lot of noise.
    It's very noisy right now.
    The animals are always hungry
       at sunrise.

2　Mrs. Jones is cooking dinner.
　　Mr. Jones worked all day long.
　　He comes home at sunset.
　　The food comes from the farm.
　　Fresh food is very healthy.

cousin	the child of your aunt or uncle
	I invited my aunts, uncles, and cousins to the picnic.
to make money	to get money from a job or from work
	My cousin has an interesting job, but he doesn't make a lot of money.
to breathe	to take air into the body
	Fish can breathe under water, but people have to breathe air.
dirty	This shirt is dirty.

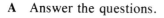

A　Answer the questions.

1　Where does Mrs. Jones live?
2　What is she feeding?
3　Are the other animals hungry, too?
4　Are they making a lot of noise?
5　Is it quiet now?
6　When are the animals hungry?
7　Who is cooking dinner?
8　How long did Mr. Jones work?
9　When does he come home?

10   Where does the food come from?
11   Is fresh food healthy?
12   Do you have many cousins?
13   Do you make a lot of money?
14   Do you breathe fast when you're excited?

B Answer the questions. Use the cues.

1   Who is feeding the animals? *the farmer*
2   Is that dress clean? *no, dirty*
3   Is the city noisier than the country? *yes*
4   What time did you get up this morning? *before sunrise*
5   Does Nancy like to cook? *no*

STRUCTURE

The past progressive tense

Affirmative forms

A **Repeat.**
I was talking.
He was reading.
She was driving.

B **Substitute.**

Mr. Dale was	sleeping.
	sitting.
	cooking.
	leaving.

Diane	
I	
The boss	was calling the office.
Ms. Learson	

C **Answer.**
Was Mr. Cole sleeping?
Was Miss Simpson working?
Was the child playing?
Was the teacher writing?
Was the horse eating?
Was Mrs. Bell reading the newspaper?
Was she looking for something?
Was it snowing yesterday?
Was it raining Monday?

D Follow the model.

> Are you typing now? →
> No, I was typing an hour ago.

Are you helping the children now?
Are you watching television now?
Are you studying now?
Are you having trouble now?
Are you listening to music now?

E Repeat.
They were walking.
We were studying.
You were reading.

F Substitute.

The men were	sleeping.
	running.
	pushing.
	rushing.
	eating.

We	
They	
You	were waiting for the train.
You and I	
The women	

G Answer.
Were the students writing?
Were they studying English?
Were you and Bill swimming?
Were we typing fast?
Was I playing well?
Was I winning?
Were the tourists waiting for him?
Were they watching the traffic?
Were you and Mary feeding the animals?

H Follow the model.

> Is Mrs. Gibson reading today? →
> Yes. She was reading yesterday, too.

Is Mr. Jennings wearing a hat today?
Are the children playing football today?
Am I talking too fast today?

Is the traffic making noise today?
Are the trains running late today?
Is it raining today?
Are you and Helen waiting for Tom today?
Is the car running all right today?

SUMMARY

I am reading now.
I was reading yesterday.

She is swimming now.
She was swimming an hour ago.

It is snowing now.
It was snowing this morning.

We are having lunch now.
We were having lunch at noon.

You are typing fast today.
You were typing fast yesterday.

They are traveling around the world.
They were traveling around the world last month.

Writing Practice

A Complete the sentences with the past progressive form of the verbs.

1 (talk)   We _____ on the telephone.
2 (visit)   Our friends _____ us.
3 (stand)   Mrs. Franklin _____ near the door.
4 (watch)   Nobody _____ the children.
5 (write)   The students _____ in their books.
6 (explain)   Pat and I _____ the lesson.
7 (help)   You and Tina _____ the teacher.
8 (wait)   I _____ for you.
9 (play)   You _____ tennis very well.
10 (examine)   The doctor _____ the man.

B Answer the questions according to the cues. Follow the model.

What were you doing last night? *read a book →*
I was reading a book.

1 What was Ms. Carney doing last night? *write letters*
2 What was I doing last Sunday? *swim*
3 What were the Smiths doing yesterday? *have a picnic*
4 What were you and Alan doing last night? *watch television*
5 What were you doing last week? *work*
6 What were the students doing yesterday? *study history*
7 What was the tour guide doing yesterday? *plan a trip*
8 What was I doing this morning? *explain how to use the machine*

On a farm

Negative forms of the past progressive tense

A **Repeat.**
She was not working.
They were not studying.
I was not driving.

B **Substitute.**

He	
I	
She	was not reading.
Bill	
The teacher	

They	
We	
You	were not saying anything.
You and I	
The doctors	

C Answer. Use *no*.

Was Bob shopping?
Were they sitting here?
Were you taking pills?
Were we playing tennis Wednesday?
Was the bus leaving?
Were the men laughing?
Was the plane landing?
Were you and Clara looking for a job?
Was Mr. Ramos meeting them?
Was I talking too much?

D Follow the models.

He was not playing. →
He wasn't playing.

They were not reading. →
They weren't reading.

I was not living at home.
You were not selling enough.
We were not moving.
Ronald and I were not carrying cash.
Mrs. Simpson was not calling you.
They were not changing planes.
You and Thelma were not doing anything.
My friends were not going with me.
The dentist was not drilling.
He was not delivering the mail.

E Answer. Use *no* and the contraction. Follow the model.

Was he drinking coffee? →
No, he wasn't drinking coffee.

Were they coming by bus?
Were you working at home?
Was Ms. Clark cooking?
Was I losing?
Were the boys playing soccer?
Were the children riding bicycles?
Was George reading the newspaper?
Were you and Bob making a deposit?
Was Eleanor looking for a doctor?
Were we driving too fast?
Were you opening the door?
Was Carl preparing dinner?
Were they reading?

SUMMARY

I was eating.   *affirmative*
I was not eating.   *negative*
I wasn't eating.   *negative*

We were working.   *affirmative*
We were not working.   *negative*
We weren't working.   *negative*

Writing Practice

Change the sentences from the affirmative to the negative. Follow the model.

He was playing. →
He was not playing.
He wasn't playing.

1 Bob was sleeping.
   Bob _____ sleeping.
   Bob _____ sleeping.
2 The doctor was examining Mr. Molson.
   The doctor _____ examining Mr. Molson.
   The doctor _____ examining Mr. Molson.
3 They were standing up.
   They _____ standing up.
   They _____ standing up.
4 The machine was running well.
   The machine _____ running well.
   The machine _____ running well.
5 The train was stopping.
   The train _____ stopping.
   The train _____ stopping.
6 The plane was turning.
   The plane _____ turning.
   The plane _____ turning.
7 We were whispering.
   We _____ whispering.
   We _____ whispering.
8 You were checking the machines.
   You _____ checking the machines.
   You _____ checking the machines.

Comparison of adjectives: *as . . . as*

A   Repeat.

This blouse is as beautiful as that one.
I am as old as Peter.
New York is as noisy as Hong Kong.

B   Substitute.

This city is as
| large |
| crowded |
| old |
| exciting |
as that one.

John was as
| weak |
| quiet |
| funny |
| bad |
| strong |
as Margaret.

C   Answer. Follow the model.

Is Ted older than Pete? →
No, Pete is as old as Ted.

Are the boys bigger than the girls?
Is the boss busier than the secretary?
Is Jack healthier than Oliver?
Is the book more boring than the movie?
Is your house colder than Bob's house?
Is this class more crowded than our class?
Is your car faster than Ellen's car?
Are they nicer than Bob and Tim?

SUMMARY

big   This house is big. That house is big.
        This house is as big as that house.

hot   The coffee is hot. The tea is hot.
        The coffee is as hot as the tea.

The city never sleeps.

Writing Practice

Follow the model.

> Mary is tall. John is tall, too. →
> John is as tall as Mary.

1 The shirts are expensive. The skirts are expensive, too.
2 The airport is large. The train station is large, too.
3 The women are happy. The men are happy, too.
4 The truck is old. The car is old, too.
5 Sam was nice. Linda was nice, too.
6 The Hinkles were busy. We were busy, too.
7 My trip was long. Your trip was long, too.
8 The meat is delicious. The vegetables are delicious, too.
9 Your clothes are wet. Her clothes are wet, too.
10 Alice and Carol are healthy. The boys are healthy, too.
11 The train is fast. The bus is fast, too.
12 Freddy is weak. Gary is weak, too.
13 That statue is beautiful. This statue is beautiful, too.
14 Baseball is exciting. Football is exciting, too.
15 The parents are hungry. The children are hungry, too.

Infinitive phrases

A Repeat.

Ask Mrs. Adams to help you.
I told him to stop the car.
They want me to wait for them.

B Substitute.

| The boss | hired
wanted
told
asked | me to type letters. |

| We | chose
invited
sent
wanted | him to talk to the group. |

C Answer.

Do you want Miss Gore to plan a meeting?
Did you want Mrs. Scott to bring the report?
Did Mr. Seaver ask you to play tennis?
Did he invite you to have lunch with him?
Did the boss hire someone to finish the work?
Did you tell your cousin to feed the animals?
Did they send someone to help you?
Did the teacher choose a student to write a story?
Did they ask you to fill out a form?
Did you tell the children to be quiet?

In the country

14

SUMMARY

| want |
| hire |
| tell |
| ask | someone to do something |
| choose |
| invite |
| send |

I want her to help me.
They told me to wait here.
Ask the doctor to check your throat.

Writing Practice

A Follow the model.

> Mr. Carpenter is helping the tourists. →
> Did you ask him to help the tourists?

1 The waiter is bringing coffee.
2 Mrs. Fox is answering the letter.
3 The children are playing outside.
4 Sam is buying two newspapers.
5 Ellen is washing the car.

B Write sentences. Follow the model.

> Miss Foster / invite / me / stay with her. →
> Miss Foster invited me to stay with her.

1 The teacher / choose / Miss Lamb / answer the question.
2 The company / hire / someone / operate the machine.
3 The hospital / send / a nurse / take my blood pressure.
4 I / want / you / leave immediately.
5 My boss / ask / me / go on a business trip.
6 We / tell / the salesman / come back at five o'clock.
7 I / want / my cousin / cook dinner.
8 Mr. Matthews / tell / me / reserve a room.

VERB PRACTICE

to pick something up
to pick up something
to pick it up

to turn something on
to turn on something
to turn it on

to listen to something
to listen to it

A   Answer.

Did Joe pick up the tickets?
Did he pick them up?
Did you pick up the brochure at the agency?
Did you pick it up?
Can you pick the car up?
Can you pick it up?
Can the children pick the table up?
Can they pick it up?

Did Lorna turn the radio on?
Did she turn it on?
Did Allen turn the heater on?
Did he turn it on?
Did you turn on the windshield wipers?
Did you turn them on?
Did you turn on the light?
Did you turn it on?

Is Laura listening to the radio?
Is she listening to it?
Do the students listen to their teachers?
Do they listen to them?
Do you listen to music?
What do you listen to?

B   Follow the models.

Please turn the radio on. →
Please turn it on.

Please pick up the brochures. →
Please pick them up.

Please turn the headlights on.
Please turn on the light.

Please pick the stamps up.
Please pick up the phone book.
Please listen to Miss Nelson.
Please listen to the news story.

READING

The country cousins

My name is William. Last week I was in the country. I was visiting my cousins. They live on a farm. My first morning on the farm I got up late.

"I didn't see you this morning. Were you and Sara sleeping?" I asked my cousin Alfred.

"Oh, no," he answered. "We get up very early here. This morning at five o'clock you were sleeping, but we were working."

"What were you doing at five o'clock in the morning?" I asked.

"I was feeding the animals. Sara was cooking."

"Poor Alfred," I thought. Life is hard. "Do you always have to work so much?" I asked.

"We work hard from sunrise to sunset. But we enjoy it."

"Do you make a lot of money?"

"No. But we don't need much money. Most of our food comes from the farm. It's fresh and good. We don't have to travel to work. We don't need fancy clothes for work. We have enough money."

"And you don't pay for nice, fresh air," I said.

"When you were at home in the city," said Alfred, "you were breathing dirty air. Here we always breathe good, clean air. The city is too noisy, too. When we visited you in the city, we didn't sleep. All night long the cars and trucks were making noise. It's quiet here. We like the country. The country is better than the city."

Alfred and his family are very healthy. Alfred is as strong as a horse. But Alfred is wrong. The city was too noisy for Alfred, but the country was too quiet for me. When Alfred was talking about the country, I was thinking about the city. There is always something to do in the city. At nine o'clock every night Alfred and his family were sleeping. In the city some people were working. Other people were eating or visiting the theater. People were getting on or off buses or taxis or trains or planes. In the city people were doing things. In the country my cousins were sleeping.

Do you know what I was doing? Nothing. I was breathing fresh air. It was healthy but it was boring. Alfred is wrong. The city is better than the country. What do you think?

Questions

1. Where was William last week?
2. Who was he visiting?
3. Did he get up late the first morning?
4. Who was working at five o'clock?
5. What was Alfred doing?
6. What was Sara doing?
7. How long do Sara and Alfred work every day?
8. Do they enjoy hard work?
9. Do they make a lot of money?
10. Do they need much money?
11. Where does most of their food come from?
12. How is their food?
13. Do they pay to travel to work?
14. Do they need fancy clothes for work?
15. Do they have enough money?
16. How is the air in the city?
17. How is the air in the country?
18. Does Alfred say the city is too noisy?
19. Did Sara and Alfred sleep in the city?
20. What were the cars and trucks doing in the city?
21. Where is it quiet?
22. How is Alfred? Is he strong?

23 What were Alfred and his family doing at nine o'clock?
24 Were people working in the city?
25 What else were people doing in the city?
26 What was William doing?
27 Does William like the country?

Personal Questions
1 Do you live in the city or the country?
2 Do you work in the city or the country?
3 Do you think the city is as nice as the country?
4 Do you think the country is healthier than the city?
5 Is the country as exciting as the city?
6 What do you do when you go to the city (country)?

LESSON REVIEW

I Complete the sentences.

cousin	breathe	as	cook	sunrise
farm	noisy	feed	dirty	noise

1 I got up very early today—an hour before _____ .
2 Please don't make so much _____ . I want to hear the radio.
3 They have animals on the _____ .
4 He is my _____ . His father is my father's brother.
5 Jane is _____ tall as Michael.
6 I like to _____ good, clean air.
7 Everybody is talking. It is very _____ .
8 The animals are hungry. Let's _____ them.
9 I'm always in the kitchen. I _____ a lot.
10 Please wash the car. It's _____ .

II Answer the questions. Follow the model.

Is he talking now? →
No, but he was talking earlier.

1 Is she combing her hair now?
2 Are the children writing now?
3 Am I winning now?
4 Is Bob using the machine now?
5 Are the boys washing the car now?
6 Is the dentist taking x rays now?
7 Is Ellen studying now?
8 Are they cooking dinner now?
9 Are they following us now?
10 Are we reading well now?

III Follow the model.

John works hard. →
He wasn't working hard this morning!

1 Miss Blair drives fast.
2 Mr. Lewis speaks seriously.
3 The children play quietly.
4 The secretaries type fast.
5 That football player runs fast.

IV Follow the model.

Is this car faster than that car? →
No, that car is as fast as this car.

1 Is the train safer than the plane?
2 Is your school more modern than my school?
3 Are the magazines more interesting than the newspapers?
4 Is the boss busier than the secretary?
5 Is Allen stronger than Vicky?

V Answer the questions according to the cues. Follow the model.

What did you tell Albert? *feed the animals* →
I told him to feed the animals.

1 What did you tell the students? *study the lesson*
2 What did you ask the mechanic? *check the oil*
3 Do you want me to type the letter? *yes*
4 Who did you hire to answer correspondence? *Mrs. Carney*
5 Did you invite someone to stay tonight? *yes, Ann and Bill*

VI You are Alfred or Sara. Answer the questions and tell a story.

Where do you live?
Do you have a family?
What time do you get up in the morning?
What work do you do?
Do you make a lot of money?
Do you go to bed early?
Do you ever visit the city?
What is it like in the city?
Which do you like better, the country or the city?

LESSON 2

NEW WORDS

1 Mr. Chapman is an overseas
   operator.
   He can connect you with a
   party in a foreign country.
   One of his lines is ringing now.
   Another line rang a few
   minutes ago.

2 Mrs. Gray is using a pay
      phone.
   She is making a call.
   She already put a coin in the
      slot.
   She has an extra coin.
   She is holding the receiver and
      dialing the number.
   She is dialing direct.
   She doesn't speak to the
      operator.

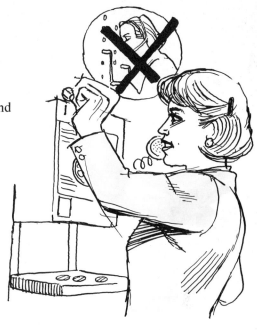

3 Miss Hale has a book shop.
   She sells expensive books and
      cheap books.
   The cheap books cost little,
      and the expensive books
      cost a lot.
   There is a big difference in
      price.

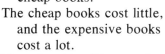

4 Miss Hale is expecting a phone
   call.
   Her cash register isn't working.
   She called the cash register
   company, and they're going
   to call her back.

person-to-person	a telephone call to one person only I want to call person-to-person to Miss Carol Leonard.
station-to-station	a telephone call to anyone at that number I'm calling this number station-to-station. I can speak to anyone.
tone	a musical noise The radio plays a tone to tell the hour.
connection	thing that connects We have a good connection. I can hear you very well.
system	a way to do things; a way to put things in groups We have a very simple filing system in the office.
token	a small thing that looks like a coin You can't use coins in that telephone. You have to use tokens.
to listen for	to wait to hear Mr. Wilkins comes home every day at 5:10. At 5:05 his children start to listen for his car.
busy	A telephone line is busy when someone is using it. I tried to call the Lindens, but their line was busy.

free not busy
You can use the phone now; it's free.

up over, finished (of time)
I rented the machine for one hour, and the time is almost up.

Pardon me. Pardon me, sir. Can you tell me the time?

Here. Do you want this piece of candy? Here, take it.

A Answer the questions.

1   What is Mr. Chapman?
2   Can he connect you with a party in a foreign country?
3   What is ringing now?
4   Who is using a pay phone?
5   What is she making?
6   Where did she put a coin?
7   Does she have an extra coin?
8   What is she holding?
9   Is she dialing the number?
10 Is she dialing direct?
11 Does she speak to the operator?
12 What does Miss Hale have?
13 What kind of books does she sell?
14 How much do the books cost?
15 Is there a big difference in price between the cheap books and the expensive books?
16 Who is expecting a phone call?
17 Is the cash register working?
18 Who is going to call her back?

B Answer the questions. Use the cues.

1   Is a station-to-station call cheaper than a person-to-person call? *yes*
2   Does that country have a modern telephone system? *no*
3   Where can I buy tokens for the telephone? *in the post office*
4   What do you want me to listen for? *the phone*
5   Was the lawyer's line free? *yes*

COMPARISON
OF
DIALS

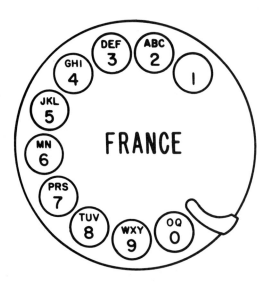

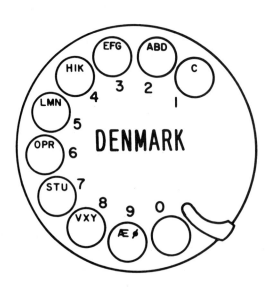

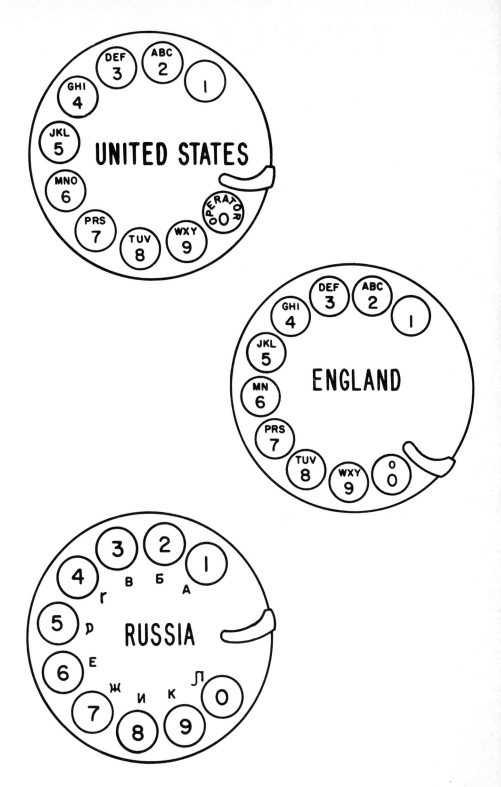

Making a call

STRUCTURE

Possessive pronouns *his, hers, theirs*

His

A   Repeat.
That book is John's.
That book is his.

I have Mr. Gray's report.
I have his report.
I have his.

B   Follow the models.

This coat is Mr. Hansen's. →
This coat is his.

This secretary is Mr. Barrett's.
These files are Mr. Warden's.

This team is John's.
That house is Martin's.
This book is the boy's.
The clothing store is Mr. Hodge's.
The calculator is Mr. Prince's.
That wallet is Peter's.

Do you have Mr. Lee's report? →
No, the secretary has his.

Do you have Mr. Heller's files?
Do you have Allen's typewriter?
Do you have Mr. Seaver's calculator?
Do you have Tom's newspaper?
Do you have Mr. Green's photographs?

Hers

A   Repeat.
Is this Mrs. Teller's application?
No, that one is hers.

Her file is in your office.
Hers is in your office.

B   Follow the models.

Is this Mrs. Brown's application? →
No, that one is hers.

Is this Miss Ross's shop?
Is this her letter?
Is this Mrs. Bishop's hat?
Is this her package?
Is this Mrs. Carter's bicycle?
Is this her seat?
Is this her tour group?

Are these Miss Wright's postcards? →
No, hers are on the table.

Are these Miss Hayne's reports?
Are these her letters?
Are these Mrs. Town's coins?
Are these her tokens?
Are these Miss Laver's paintings?
Are these her photographs?
Are these her scissors?
Are these Ms. Christie's books?

Theirs

A   Repeat.
The Anderson's car is yellow.
Their car is yellow.
Theirs is yellow.
Those suitcases are theirs.

B   Answer. Use *yes.*
Are those books theirs?
Is that telephone theirs?
Is that little boy theirs?
Is that building theirs?
Are the reports theirs?
Is the green bus theirs?
Are those bicycles theirs?
Are these clients theirs?

C   Follow the model.

>Whose tickets does she have? →
>She has theirs.

Whose report do you have?
Whose invitation does he have?
Whose radio do I have?
Whose tools do you have?
Whose magazine does she have?

D   Follow the models.

>It's their book. →
>It's theirs.

>This is her house. →
>This is hers.

>Here are their reports. →
>Here are theirs.

I read his book.
That's their house.
We saw her x ray.
They know his work.
Here are her prescriptions.
Where are their passbooks?
He has her check.
I have their luggage.
This is his application.

Is this Mary's car? →
Yes, it's hers.

Is that Phil's and Dan's house? →
Yes, it's theirs.

Are those Bob's reports? →
Yes, they're his.

Are those Tom's children?
Is this the Smiths' bank?
Are those Mr. Burn's parents?
Is that Barbara's and Fred's shop?
Is this their suitcase?
Are those Ellen's packages?
Are those Fred's tickets?
Are those Carol's letters?
Are these Ms. Carlton's clients?

SUMMARY

The book is Frank's book.
The book is his book.
The book is his.

Miss Simpson's reports are in the file.
Her reports are in the file.
Hers are in the file.

Where is Mr. and Mrs. Allen's car?
Where is their car?
Where is theirs?

Writing Practice

A   Follow the models.

The book / Mrs. Cole →
The book is hers.

The reports / John →
The reports are his.

The house / Mr. and Mrs. Lewis →
The house is theirs.

1　The x rays　/　Mr. Davis
2　The business　/　Martha Shea
3　The newspapers　/　the boy
4　The timetable　/　the conductors
5　The clothes　/　Brad
6　The crops　/　the farmer
7　The calculator　/　Anne and Warren
8　The seats　/　the teachers
9　The savings account　/　Ms. Edmonds
10　The toothpaste　/　Billy

B　Answer with *no*. Follow the models.

Is this Bob's class? →
No, it's not his.

Are these Mrs. Gray's children? →
No, they're not hers.

1　Is this Mary's car?
2　Are these Mr. Valley's papers?
3　Is this the Brown's house?
4　Are these Mr. Edward's x rays?
5　Is this Frank's and Martha's school?
6　Are these Alice's clothes?

On the telephone

Tag endings with *isn't, is, am, aren't, are*

Isn't

A Repeat.
That book is interesting, isn't it?
Mr. Griffon is coming, isn't he?
Miss Logan is tall, isn't she?

B Ask questions. Follow the model.

> Mrs. Rider is a teacher. →
> Mrs. Rider is a teacher, isn't she?

Miss Blair is at home.
She's selling her car.
Mrs. Marks is here.
Linda is late.
Robert is sleeping.
He's a good driver.
Mr. Trent is coming back.
The boy is sick.
The plane is safe.
That house is small.
The blue car is old.
The phone is ringing.

Is

A Repeat.
John isn't leaving, is he?
The movie isn't long, is it?
She's not happy now, is she?

B Ask questions. Follow the model.

> The book isn't boring. →
> The book isn't boring, is it?

This hat isn't cheap.
The tour isn't over.
The plane isn't landing.
It isn't raining.
Mr. Trent isn't flying.
He's not here.
Mr. Redding isn't upset.
He isn't smiling.

Mrs. Hood isn't serious.
She isn't driving.
Miss Barr isn't returning.
She isn't rich.

Am

A   Repeat.
I'm not late, am I?
I'm not ready, am I?

B   Add the tag endings.
I'm not early,
I'm not strong,
I'm not sick,
I'm not typing fast,
I'm not swimming well,
I'm not making mistakes,
I'm not a good skier,

Aren't

A   Repeat.
We're leaving early, aren't we?
You're the new teacher, aren't you?
The students are learning fast, aren't they?
I'm right, aren't I?

B   Add the tag endings.
You're having trouble,
You're a tourist here,
You and Laura are studying English,
You're Ellen's brother,
We're in the right line,
We're on time,
We're winning,
Bob and I are friends,
They're arriving tonight,
The Johnsons are on vacation,
They're taking a cab,
Bill and Sue are working,
I'm on time,
I'm returning Thursday,
I'm making mistakes,
I'm talking too fast,

Are

A   Repeat.
They're not going to school, are they?
We aren't leaving yet, are we?
You're not listening, are you?

B   Add the tag endings.
You're not walking,
You and Bill aren't staying,
You're not ready,

A telephone operator

You're not working there,
Mr. Cole and I aren't too late,
We aren't hurrying,
We aren't busy,
We aren't taking the bus,
They arcn't late,
The nights aren't long now,
The waves aren't big,
Sam and Irene aren't going,

C **Add the tag endings.**
The reports are complete,
You're not busy,
Martha and I are right,
Mrs. Simmons is following us,
I'm not wrong,
It isn't snowing,
Mr. Pitney is our tour guide,
He isn't taking us to another monument,
The tourists aren't visiting the museum,
You're having lunch with Betty,
Miss Grant isn't in the office,
It's very cold outdoors,
I'm swimming fast today,
We're not going to the park,

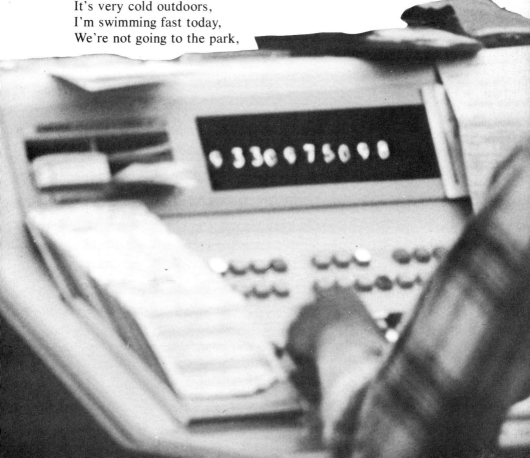

SUMMARY

He			he?
She	is . . . ,	isn't	she?
It			it?

He			he?
She	is not . . . ,	is	she?
It			it?

I	am not . . . ,		am I?

We are . . . ,			we?
You are . . . ,		aren't	you?
They are . . . ,			they?
I am . . . ,			I?

We			we?
You	are not . . . , are		you?
They			they?

She's a good teacher, isn't she?
He isn't leaving now, is he?
I'm not a good skier, am I?
You're writing the report, aren't you?
We aren't taking the train, are we?

Writing Practice

Write the correct tag endings.

1 The Jacksons are living in the country now, _____?
2 You're not happy, _____?
3 We're eating in the office today, _____?
4 Mr. Cade is calling the clients, _____?
5 Her car isn't very fast, _____?
6 I'm in the wrong line, _____?
7 Miss Peters is a good reporter, _____?
8 Mr. Wells isn't working late, _____?

38

9 I'm not a good artist, _____?
10 You're looking for the Apex file, _____?
11 The bookkeepers aren't having trouble, _____?
12 The bus is late, _____?
13 Mrs. Bowers isn't your teacher, _____?
14 Andrew and I are the oldest, _____?
15 Ms. Edwards is waiting for us, _____?
16 We're not leaving soon, _____?
17 The tokens are cheap, _____?
18 You're dialing direct, _____?
19 The new store is open for business, _____?

Comparison of adverbs

A Repeat.

Miss Boone works quietly.
Miss Rivers works more quietly than Miss Boone.
Miss Winters works the most quietly.

Mr. Field speaks seriously.
Mr. Crane speaks more seriously than Mr. Field.
Mr. Hillary speaks the most seriously.

B Follow the models.

> Does she speak seriously? →
> Yes, but I speak more seriously.

Does Helen work quickly?
Does she walk quietly?
Do the children eat hungrily?
Did the doctor leave suddenly?
Did he finish easily?
Did Mrs. Baker drive safely?
Did I answer completely?

> Does John work quietly? →
> Yes, he works the most quietly of all.

Does that pilot fly safely?
Does the girl play happily?
Do you answer seriously?
Does he arrive quickly?
Does Miss Harper swim easily?
Does Tim eat hungrily?

SUMMARY

Miss Crane works quietly.
Mrs. Jennings works more quietly than Miss Crane.
Mr. Slocum works the most quietly of the three.

Writing Practice

A Complete the sentences with the correct form of the adverbs.

1 (quickly)   Ted learns _____ than Richard.
2 (hungrily)   The children always eat lunch _____ than dinner.
3 (safely)   In our family, Bill drives the _____.
4 (easily)   Jane finished her work _____ than Beverly.
5 (quietly)   Harry speaks the _____ of all the students.

B Follow the model.

Carol plays happily. →
Ann plays more happily than Carol.
Patricia plays the most happily of the three.

1 Louis studies seriously.
   Nancy _____.
   Steve _____.
2 Walter learned to drive easily.
   Susan _____.
   Kathy _____.
3 Miss Carson drives safely.
   Mr. Hull _____.
   Mr. David _____.

Adverbs *well, better, best*

A Repeat.
David writes well.
Amy writes better than David.
Tony writes the best of all.

B   Substitute.

	drive	
The Wilsons	swim	well.
	cook	
	play	

Mr. Morgan	
The new secretary	writes better than I.
Ms. Ritter	
The teacher	

	reads	
Which student	writes	the best?
	speaks	
	studies	

C   Answer.

Does Mr. Wood write well?
Does he play the guitar well?
Does the secretary type well?
Does she work well?
Do you read well?

Does the new car run better than the old one?
Do you hear better than Miss North?
Does this machine work better than that one?
Does our team play better than theirs?
Do you cook better than your parents?

Does Miss Paine speak the best?
Does she write the best?
Does the tall boy swim the best?
Does he run the best?
Do you drive the best in your family?

SUMMARY

Miss Ritter reads well.
Mr. Howard reads better than Miss Ritter.
Mrs. York reads the best of the three.

Writing Practice

Follow the model.

> Mr. Porter speaks well. →
> Miss Harvey speaks better than Mr. Porter.
> Mr. Drew speaks the best of the three.

1 Miss Douglas writes well.
  Mr. Baldwin _____ .
  Ms. Beckett _____ .
2 The yellow car runs well.
  The blue car _____ .
  The green car _____ .
3 My camera works well.
  Miss Chase's camera _____ .
  Your camera _____ .
4 Your team plays well.
  My team _____ .
  Mr. Dawson's team _____ .
5 Mr. Curtis rides a bicycle well.
  Miss Gibbs _____ .
  Mr. Farmer _____ .

Telephone operators

VERB PRACTICE

to put in something
to put something in
to put it in

to take out something
to take something out
to take it out

A   Answer.

Did the mechanic put the oil in?
Did he put it in?
Did you put the coins in?
Did you put them in?

Did Sara put in the new token?
Did she put it in?
Did Mrs. Lester put in the fresh roll of film?
Did she put it in?

Did the children take the candy out?
Did they take it out?
Did they take the bicycles out?
Did they take them out?

Did you take out the old heater?
Did you take it out?
Did you take out the blue seats?
Did you take them out?

B   Follow the models.

Don't put the oil in now. →
Don't put it in now.

Don't take out the old oil. →
Don't take it out.

Don't put the money in.
Don't take the horse out.
Don't put the coins in.
Don't take the food out.
Don't take out the large cups.
Don't put in the small tokens.

CONVERSATION

Pay Phones

Man   Pardon me, miss. How does this telephone work? Where do I put in the coins?

Woman   The phones don't take coins. You need a special token.

Man   Where can I buy tokens?

Woman   All the shops sell them. They cost very little. But here, I have an extra one. Take it.

Man   Thank you very much.

Woman   Now, pick up the receiver. Put the token in the slot. Listen for the tone.

Man   I hear the tone. Now what do I do?

Woman   Now dial your number. Is the phone ringing?

Man   Yes, but no one is answering.

Woman   If no one answers, take out the token and hang up. If somebody answers, push the little button next to the token slot. That makes the connection.

Man   Thank you very much for your help.

Questions

1 Can the man use a coin in the phone?
2 What do the phones take?
3 Where can the man buy tokens?

4 Are tokens expensive?
5 What does the woman give to the man?
6 What does the man have to pick up?
7 Where does he put the token?
8 What does he listen for?
9 When he hears the tone, what does he do?
10 If nobody answers, what does he do?
11 If somebody answers, what does he do?
12 What happens when he pushes the button?

Personal Questions

1 Do you have a telephone at home?
2 Do you dial your calls or do you call the operator?
3 Do you ever call overseas?
4 What is your telephone number?
5 Is telephone service expensive?
6 Are there public telephones where you live?
7 Do public telephones take coins or tokens? How much does a call cost?

READING

An overseas call

Operator Overseas Operator Number 16. Can I help you?

Man Yes, please. I dialed my friend's number. You connected me. But the number wasn't his. It was a wrong number. It's all right to dial direct, isn't it?

45

Operator	Where are you calling, sir?
Man	The Republic of Saint Clement.
Operator	I'm sorry, sir. You can't dial direct to Saint Clement. But I can connect you. What is your number, please, and your friend's number?
Man	My number is 773-7294. His is 22-17-3. They're working on a direct-dial system in Saint Clement, aren't they?
Operator	Yes, they are. They started last year. It takes time. Do you want to call person-to-person or station-to-station?
Man	What's the difference?
Operator	With person-to-person you don't have to pay if your party isn't there. With station-to-station you pay if anybody answers. Station-to-station is much cheaper.
Man	Station-to-station is OK. My friend is expecting this call.
Operator	Sir, the line is busy. Please hang up. I have your number. I can call you back when the line is free.
	(A few minutes later)
Operator	Sir, I have your party on the line.
Man	It's the right number this time, isn't it?
Operator	Yes, it is, 22-17-3. The charge is two-twenty for the first three minutes.
Man	Operator, please tell me when the three minutes are up.
Operator	Yes, sir. Your party is on. Go ahead, please.
Man	Thank you. Hello, Sebastian? This is Michael. How are you?

Questions

1 What kind of operator is speaking?
2 What is the operator's number?
3 What number did the man dial?
4 Did they connect him?
5 Was the number his friend's number?
6 Was it a wrong number?
7 Does the man want to dial direct?
8 Where is the man calling?
9 Can you dial direct to Saint Clement?
10 Can the operator connect the man with Saint Clement?
11 What does the operator ask for?
12 What is the man's number?
13 Whose number is 22-17-3?
14 Are they working on a direct-dial system in Saint Clement?
15 When did they start?
16 Which is more expensive, person-to-person or station-to-station?
17 Does the man choose person-to-person or station-to-station?
18 Why can't the man talk to Saint Clement right away?
19 Does the operator call the man back?
20 What is the charge for three minutes?

A modern telephone

LESSON REVIEW

I Complete the conversation with words from the list.

busy	aren't	pay
calls	party	well
up	coins	person-to-person
isn't	system	free

"Mrs. Blake, you're a telephone operator, _____ you?"

"Yes, I am."

"What do you do at work?"

"Well, I help people make telephone _____. They call me when they want to call someone _____. I connect them with their _____. Sometimes the line is _____. Then I have to call them back when it's _____. When people are calling from a _____ phone, I tell them how many _____ to use. I also tell them when their three minutes are _____."

"I'm sure you know the telephone _____ very _____. Your job is interesting, _____ it?"

"Yes, it is. I like it very much."

II Change the words in italics to *his, hers,* or *theirs.*

I have *her book.* →
I have hers.

1   We saw *their house.*
2   Mary bought *Bill's jacket.*
3   Nobody saw *their x rays.*
4   Did you look at *Mr. and Mrs. Harper's pictures?*
5   We liked *Jane's children.*
6   They sold *their coins.*
7   Albert kept *his coins.*
8   Mrs. Wilson sold *her car.*
9   We washed *their clothes.*
10 Sam read *Joan's story.*

47

III Write the correct tag endings.

He is tall, _____ ? →
He is tall, isn't he?

1 The tour guides are nice, _____ ?
2 We aren't late, _____ ?
3 You aren't upset, _____ ?
4 We're early, _____ ?
5 The reports aren't complete, _____ ?
6 He isn't your brother, _____ ?
7 I'm not speaking to the operator, _____ ?
8 You and Sam are coming, _____ ?
9 Miss Day is going to the dentist, _____ ?
10 I'm early, _____ ?
11 It isn't too cold, _____ ?
12 She isn't our tour guide, _____ ?
13 Mr. Baird is a good driver, _____ ?
14 This copier isn't new, _____ ?

IV Complete the sentences with the correct form of the adverbs.

1 (well) Mr. Lee swims _____ than Mr. Arnold.
2 (quickly) Miss Grayson finished the report _____ than I.
3 (quietly) Of all the tour guides, Mr. Williams speaks _____ .
4 (well) Marilyn Wayne writes _____ of all the students.
5 (well, well) Mrs. Billings cooks very _____ , but you cook _____ than she.
6 (safely) The police officers drive _____ than I.
7 (hungrily) Of all the children, Kenneth ate _____ .
8 (well) We all read well, but the teacher reads _____ .

V Write a conversation between Mr. Peterson and a telephone operator. Use the information below.

Mr. Peterson calls the operator and says hello. He tells her he is having trouble calling his friend. Every time he dials the number, the line is busy. He asks the operator if there is something wrong with the telephone line. The operator tells him she has to check. She asks him what number he is calling. He tells her 726-4113. The operator thanks him and tells him to hold on, please. Mr. Peterson explains that he can't understand it—his friend never talks long on the phone. The operator asks him if he has the right number. Mr. Peterson says he thinks so, but he can check it in the phone book. Then he tells the operator he found the number in the phone book, and it is 726-4112. He says he is sorry. The operator says that's all right, and then they both say good-bye.

LESSON 3

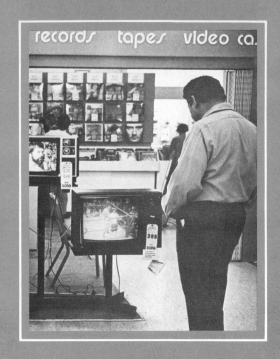

NEW WORDS

1   Miss Payne has a small TV set.
It has a small screen and a big
    antenna.
She's watching a cultural
    program on channel 3.
The sound is very good.
Television brings entertainment
    into the home.

2   Mr. Cummings works in a
       factory.
    He is teaching a new employee.
    The employee doesn't
       remember what to do.
    He is holding part of a
       telephone.

3   In the old days, newsreels were
       very popular.
    People saw news events from
       all over the world.
    They saw life in remote places.
    Newsreels taught people a lot.

NEWS OF THE WEEK

midnight   twelve o'clock at night
I'm always in bed before midnight.

choice   a number of things to choose from
You have a choice of colors.

roof   That house has no
television antenna
on the roof.

opinion   what someone thinks or believes about something
What's your opinion of Mrs. Hasting's report?

to become   to come to be
I had lunch six hours ago. I'm becoming hungry again.
Past tense: became
Television became popular in the 1950s.

early   not new or modern; the first
The early cars were slow and noisy.

at first   in the beginning
At first he wrote to us often, but now he's too busy to write.

far away   not near
Japan is far away from Canada.

to have in mind   to think of
We have many cars for sale here. What did you have in
mind—a small one or a big one?

A   Answer the questions.

1   Who has a small TV set?
2   Does the television have a big screen?
3   Does it have a big antenna?
4   What is Miss Payne watching?
5   What channel is it on?
6   How is the sound?
7   What does television bring into the home?
8   Where does Mr. Cummings work?
9   Who is he teaching?
10   Does the employee remember what to do?
11   What is he holding?
12   When were newsreels very popular?
13   What did people see?
14   Did they see life in remote places?
15   Last night, did you go to bed before or after midnight?

16 Is your television antenna on the set or on the roof?
17 In your opinion, is English easy?
18 Does anyone write to you from far away?

B Answer the questions. Use the cues.

1 Do you remember Miss Warren's address? *no*
2 When did he finish the painting? *last night at midnight*
3 Is that what you had in mind? *yes*
4 Where is television popular? *all over the world*
5 What are you watching? *a news program*
6 What channel is it on? *channel 4*
7 Where does Mrs. Grover teach? *in the Madison School*

STRUCTURE

Possessive pronouns *mine, yours, ours*

Mine

A Repeat.
This is my car. It's mine.
John's house is big, but mine is small.

B Follow the models.

Is this your book? →
Yes, it's mine.

Is this your camera?
Is this your bicycle?
Is this your calculator?
Is this your guitar?
Is this your umbrella?

Are these your letters? →
Yes, they're mine.

Are these your keys?
Are these your tools?
Are these your photographs?
Are these your cigarettes?
Are these your coins?

My car is green. →
Really? Mine is, too.

My house is near the university.
My brother is a bookkeeper.
My television set is portable.
My daughter is a very good skier.
My secretary is excellent.

Yours

A   Repeat.
This isn't my copy. It's yours.
My phone doesn't work. Can I use yours?

B   Follow the models.

Whose mail is that? →
I think it's yours.

Whose passbook is that?
Whose check is that?
Whose napkin is that?
Whose newspaper is that?
Whose shampoo is that?

Antennas

Are these your keys? →
No, they're yours.

Are these your scissors?
Are these your magazines?
Are these your deposit slips?
Are these your envelopes?
Are these your stamps?

We need a car. →
Let's use yours.

We need a camera.
We need an office.
We need a desk.
We need a lawyer.
We need a boat.

Ours

A Repeat.

It's our house. It's ours.
Their children are younger than ours.

B Follow the models.

Which house is yours? →
That one is ours.

Which car is yours?
Which travel agency is yours?
Which tour guide is yours?
Which radio is yours?
Which suitcase is yours?
Which office is yours?

We have an old stadium. →
Yes. It's older than ours.

We have old suitcases. →
Yes. They're older than ours.

We have an old swimming pool.
We have an old television set.
We have old bicycles.
We have an old farm.
We have old stores.
We have an old clock.
We have old cash registers.

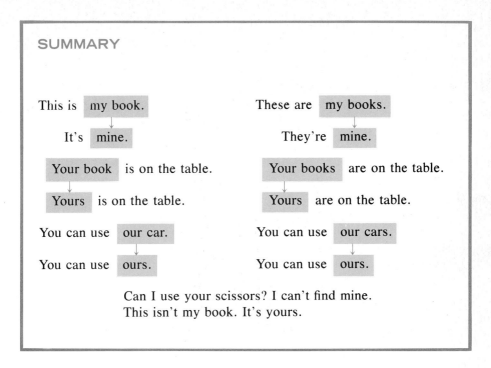

This is my book.

It's mine.

Your book is on the table.

Yours is on the table.

You can use our car.

You can use ours.

These are my books.

They're mine.

Your books are on the table.

Yours are on the table.

You can use our cars.

You can use ours.

Can I use your scissors? I can't find mine.
This isn't my book. It's yours.

Writing Practice

A Change the sentences. Follow the model.

> This is my comb. →
> This comb is mine.

1 This is your report.
2 These are our photographs.
3 That's my umbrella.
4 Those are our magazines.
5 That's your driver's license.
6 That's my wallet.

B Complete the sentences. Use *mine, yours,* or *ours.*

1 I have a ticket. The ticket is _____.
2 You and Joan have a new mirror. The mirror is _____.
3 Ed and I have a beautiful picture. The picture is _____.
4 You have tax forms. The tax forms are _____.
5 I have stamps. The stamps are _____.
6 We have a checking account. The account is _____.

Expressions with *many* and *much*

How many

A   Repeat.
How many channels are there?
I don't know how many shirts he has.
How many tickets do you want?

B   Ask.
Ask a student how many credit cards he has.
Ask a student how many copies she needs.
Ask a student how many batteries he wants.
Ask a student how many suitcases she has.
Ask a student how many rooms he needs.
Ask a student how many brothers she has.

How much

A   Repeat.
How much money does she have?
How much cream do you put in your coffee?
Tell me how much medicine he needs.

B Ask.

Ask a student how much shampoo he needs.
Ask a student how much insurance she has.
Ask a student how much gas he needs.
Ask a student how much oil she wants.
Ask a student how much soup he wants.
Ask a student how much soap she needs.

C Answer. Follow the models.

How many chairs does he have? →
I don't know how many chairs he has.

How much medicine does she need? →
I don't know how much medicine she needs.

How many tokens does he want?
How much time do you need?
How many days does Mrs. Carson need?
How much cash does she have?
How many children does he have?
How much clothing do I need?

Modern TV sets

As many . . . as, as much . . . as

A Repeat.

He drinks as much tea as I do.
The Johnsons have as many children as the Caines.

B Answer.

Does Miss Jones have as much time as Miss Ames?
Does Tokyo have as much traffic as New York?
Do you have as much work as your boss?
Do you drink as much coffee as your husband (wife)?
Do you have as many files as Mrs. Bonner?
Do I buy as many magazines as Tom?
Does Mr. Billings write as many letters as Mr. Cross?
Do your children watch as many programs as theirs?

SUMMARY

how much
as much — tea, money, time, mail

how many
as many — cups, coins, minutes, letters

How many shirts did you buy?
I bought as many shirts as John.
I don't know how much food to bring.
The car doesn't use as much gas as the truck.

Writing Practice

A Complete the sentences. Use *many* or *much*.

1 How _____ envelopes do you need?
2 How _____ gas did you buy?
3 Do you know how _____ stamps I need for this letter?
4 Mrs. Jordan has as _____ clients as Mr. Scott.
5 You don't have as _____ insurance as we do.
6 That factory doesn't make as _____ sets as this one.
7 I don't remember how _____ film I used.
8 How _____ candy did the children eat?
9 There aren't as _____ tourists in this group as in that one.
10 We had as _____ snow this winter as last winter.

60

B Follow the model.

> I made a lot of mistakes. →
> How many mistakes did you make?

1 Dr. Collins wrote a lot of prescriptions.
2 That bus uses a lot of oil.
3 Miss Troy is visiting a lot of cities this summer.
4 Bill had a lot of cavities.
5 Mr. Simpson brought a lot of luggage with him.
6 Mrs. Miller spent a lot of time in Asia.

An early television set

Tag endings with *do, does, don't, doesn't*

Doesn't

A Repeat.

Miss Flint teaches in that school, doesn't she?
Mr. Waring has a new television set, doesn't he?
Your car uses a lot of gas, doesn't it?

B Ask questions. Follow the model.

Tom watches television often. →
Tom watches television often, doesn't he?

Mr. Sloan works late on Mondays.
Mr. Cummings works in a factory.
He knows the address.
Mrs. Grover dictates very fast.
Miss Holland takes a lot of pictures.
She goes to that museum a lot.
That bus runs often.
That factory makes radios.
That museum has a lot of sculpture.

Don't

A Repeat.

I need a new car, don't I?
You eat a lot of vegetables, don't you?
We always tip the waitress, don't we?
The Hardens usually rent a car, don't they?

B Add the tag endings.

I listen to the radio a lot,
I eat out a lot,
I usually arrive early,
You cut your daughter's hair,
You always rush home after work,
You like soccer,
We need more food,
We have an account there,
We know that man,
Mr. and Mrs. Knox have two children,
They always travel with tour groups,
The express trains run on Saturdays,

Does

A Repeat.
John doesn't know how to swim, does he?
Mrs. Miller doesn't have a television set, does she?
The bus doesn't run on Sundays, does it?

B Add the tag endings.
That train doesn't go to the city,
That school doesn't have many teachers,
That report doesn't have any mistakes,
Miss Carroll doesn't remember me,
Mrs. Bradley doesn't work on Saturdays,
Your sister doesn't like coffee,
Mr. Stewart doesn't own that store,
Your father doesn't live near you,
Mr. Page doesn't have a secretary,

Do

A Repeat.
I don't need a reservation, do I?
You don't have a checking account, do you?
We don't have time for breakfast, do we?
The Platts don't shop in the city, do they?

B Add the tag endings.
The students don't study every night,
Mr. and Mrs. Holden don't have any children,
The calculators don't need new batteries,
We don't need a new car,
We don't have any appointments this afternoon,
We don't use those forms,
You don't believe me,
You don't take cabs often,
You don't know how to type,
I don't cook very well,
I don't have to work late,
I don't have a fever,

SUMMARY

He She It	— **goes** to the city, **doesn't** —	he? she? it?
He She It	— **doesn't go** to the city, **does** —	he? she? it?
I We You They	— **go** to the city, **don't** —	I? we? you? they?
I We You They	— **don't go** to the city, **do** —	I? we? you? they?

You remember Mrs. Fox, don't you?
Mr. Armstrong doesn't have to go to the hospital, does he?
They don't watch television often, do they?
She usually eats out on Mondays, doesn't she?

Writing Practice

Complete the questions. Use *do, does, don't* or *doesn't*.

1   Miss Bentley understands the problem, _____ she?
2   You don't need my help, _____ you?
3   The students speak English well, _____ they?
4   You have a driver's license, _____ you?
5   The express train doesn't run on Sundays, _____ it?
6   We don't have enough tickets, _____ we?
7   Mr. Clifford has a new job, _____ he?
8   I have a good teacher, _____ I?
9   We need a tour guide, _____ we?
10 The students don't need new books, _____ they?

VERB PRACTICE

> to watch
> to look at
> to see

A   Substitute.

The children are watching	a football game.
	a tennis match.
	television.
	a new program.
	a good movie.

Please look at	this report.
	me.
	that picture.
	my car.
	this mistake.

Do you see	a subway station?
	the lake?
	a police officer?
	Mr. Caine often?
	the dentist every year?

B **Answer.**

Does Nancy watch television often?
Does she like to watch baseball games?
Does she like to watch cultural programs, too?
Can Tom watch the children this afternoon?
Are the children watching a football game?

Are the tourists looking at the buildings?
Do they like to look at statues and paintings?
Are the children looking at the pictures?
What are they looking at?
Are the students looking at the teacher?

Did you see the Millers last night?
Did you see that car?
Can you see the hospital from your house?
Do you have to see the doctor again?
Did you see anything interesting in the store?

READING

The small screen

How many people remember life before television? But television is not very old. True, there were television sets in the 1920s, but television became popular in the 1950s. At first television sets were very expensive. Then more people wanted sets. As factories made more sets, the prices went down. The early television sets were black-and-white only. The screens were very small. There were very few channels and very few programs. Usually there were no programs before noon or after midnight. Today, people all over the world watch and enjoy television. The screens are large. The sound is excellent. The choice of channels and programs is large. There is beautiful color, too. The television antenna is like a part of every house. There is one on every roof.

Is television good or bad? Everyone has an opinion. You have yours. I have mine. What's good about television? Television brings cheap entertainment into the home. The theater and movies are expensive; television is not. People see the news soon after it happens, on television. In the old days we waited days or weeks to see the newsreels. Satellite television brings us news and sports events from far away. Cultural programs on art, history, and music are on television. In remote areas they use television to teach.

What's wrong with television? Some children spend many hours in front of the television set. They don't read, they don't talk, they don't think. Because of television many people only watch—they don't do things. They don't play sports—they watch sports. They see and hear stories—they don't read or tell stories. They listen to the machine. They don't talk to other people. Maybe the programs are interesting—the people who watch them are not.

We have our opinion. You tell us yours.

Questions
1 Is television very old?
2 When did they invent television?
3 When did television become popular?
4 Were television sets expensive at first?
5 Did the prices go down when they made more sets?
6 How were the early television sets?
7 How were the screens?
8 Were there many channels?
9 Were there many programs?
10 Were there programs before noon or after midnight?
11 Who watches television today?
12 How are modern television sets?
13 What is there on every roof?
14 What does television bring into the home?
15 Are movies and the theater cheap?
16 When do people see the news on television?
17 How long did people wait to see newsreels?
18 What does satellite television bring us?
19 Where do they use television to teach?
20 Where do some children spend many hours?
21 When the children watch television, what don't they do?
22 What do you think of television?

Personal Questions
1 Do you have a television set at home?
2 Is your set black-and-white or color?
3 Do you have an antenna on the roof or on the set?
4 How many channels do you get?
5 What are your favorite programs?
6 When do you watch television?
7 Do you think television is good or bad for children?

LESSON REVIEW

I Complete the sentences.

mine	remember	teach	do	become	many
doesn't	factory	opinion	part	popular	ours

1 Can you _____ me to play the guitar?
2 "Is this your umbrella?" "Yes, it's _____."
3 The new employee learns fast, _____ she?
4 Sometimes television programs _____ boring if you watch them often.
5 I read a lot, but I don't have as _____ books as you.
6 You can't swim in this _____ of the lake. There is no lifeguard here.
7 The children don't know how to play soccer, _____ they?
8 What's your _____ of the new cars?
9 That's our car. The bicycle is _____, too.
10 That man was in my tour group, but I don't _____ his name.
11 Mr. Gibbons makes television antennas. He works in a _____ on Main Street.
12 Music programs on the radio are _____ all over the world.

II Choose the correct words to complete the conversation.

Harry Tom, I think you spend too (many, much) time watching television. How many programs do you watch every week?

Tom I don't think I watch as (many, much) programs as you. This is a very good news program.

Harry Well, since you're watching television, can I use your bicycle?

Tom Sure, but what happened to (you, yours)?

Harry (My, Mine) has a flat tire.

III Complete the sentences. Use *do, does, don't, doesn't, am, is, are, isn't,* or *aren't.*

1 Mrs. Thompson teaches English, _____ she?
2 Mr. Hastings is looking for a new secretary, _____ he?
3 You're not going to the city this weekend, _____ you?
4 I don't need a token for this phone, _____ I?
5 Miss Rivers doesn't like to listen to the radio, _____ she?
6 We have to reserve a room, _____ we?
7 The drugstores are open on Sundays, _____ they?
8 The Mortons usually eat out on Saturdays, _____ they?
9 He's not getting nervous, _____ he?
10 You don't remember me, _____ you?

IV Write a short paragraph about your favorite television program. Write at least four sentences.

LESSON 4

NEW WORDS

1 Mr. and Mrs. Lewis are at the airport.
They're going to a foreign country.
They're very excited.
They have their tickets and passports.
The porter has their luggage.
He will take care of it.

2 Miss Peters and Miss Steele are
      both teachers.
   They're in the same profession.
   They're traveling together
      because they have similar
      interests.
   That is their reason for
      traveling together.
   Miss Peters has a number of
      brochures.
   She and Miss Steele are
      looking them over.

3 Mr. Sands is going to a tropical
      island.
   He is joining a tour group.
   He has to pay in advance.
   It is a complete package tour.
   Even meals are included.

4   Mr. and Mrs. Reed are
      planning a vacation.
    Mr. Reed wants to go sight-
      seeing.
    Mrs. Reed prefers to relax on a
      beach somewhere.
    She needs a rest.

rule	the right way to do something or to play a game I like football, but I don't know all the rules of the game.
fact	something that is true I know a little about what happened, but I don't know all the facts.
maid	a woman who works in a hotel and cleans the rooms Please ask the maid to leave more towels in the room.
strange	new; describing something that you don't know or know about What was that strange sound?
either	any more than another I know you don't like that program. I don't like it either.
to let someone know	to tell him or her Please let me know if you can come with me tomorrow. *Past tense:* let know She let me know the address.

A   Answer the questions.

1   Where are the Lewises going?
2   Are they excited?
3   Do they have their passports?
4   Who has their luggage?
5   Who will take care of it?
6   Are Miss Peters and Miss Steele both teachers?
7   Are they in the same profession?
8   Why are they traveling together?
9   What does Miss Peters have?
10   Is she looking them over?
11   Where is Mr. Sands going?
12   Is he joining a tour group?
13   When does he have to pay?
14   Are meals included in the package tour?
15   What does Mr. Reed like to do?
16   What does Mrs. Reed prefer to do?
17   What does she need?
18   How many maids work in the hotel?
19   Do you know what that strange machine is?
20   Do you let your husband (wife) know when you're going to be late?

B   Rewrite the sentences. Use *both*.

1   They're _____ very excited.
2   They were _____ sick last week.
3   They're _____ taking the late flight.
4   They're _____ joining a tour group.
5   They can _____ leave at five o'clock.
6   They can _____ stay at the Westport Hotel.
7   They _____ know how to drive.
8   They _____ work in the city.

STRUCTURE

The future tense

Declarative sentences

A   **Repeat.**
I will leave next week.
You will like the new restaurant.
Miss Collins will be on vacation next month.
We will see you Monday.
The Gordons will return tomorrow night.

B Answer.

Will Mr. Sherman be here next week?
Will he finish the work?
Will he have time?

Will Mrs. Payne enjoy the group tour?
Will she go sight-seeing?
Will she meet many people?

Will it rain tomorrow?
Will it be cold?

Will the nurses know what to do?
Will they bring the medicine?
Will they call the doctor?

Will you take care of the tickets?
Will you remember the passports?
Will you travel by plane?

Will I have to get up early?
Will I understand the tour guides?
Will we like the island?
Will we have good weather?

Will you and Mr. Hodge travel together?
Will you go sight-seeing?
Will you need reservations?

On vacation

C Follow the model.

>Do I need more money? →
>No, but you will need more money tomorrow.

Do I have time to relax?
Do we have to stop for gas?
Does Miss Brown need the report?
Does Mr. Edwards understand the rules?
Do the students need a rest?
Do they have to work late?

SUMMARY

work	I work every day.
(go, help, begin)	I worked yesterday.
	I am working now.
	I will work tomorrow.
be	The stores are crowded today.
	They were crowded yesterday.
	They will be crowded tomorrow.

The tour will begin in five minutes.
The secretary will type the report next week.
The weather will be good tomorrow.

HAWAII
Privacy in Paradise

CAYMAN ISLANDS
VACATIONS

Destination
Bahamas

Palmas del Mar
The Mediterranean Side of Puerto Rico

One Week Caribbean Air/Sea Cruises

Rates

an Plus

lines

Writing Practice

A Complete the sentences with the future tense form of the verbs.

1 (examine) The doctor ＿＿ you in a few minutes.
2 (fly) Captain Drake ＿＿ this plane next Thursday.
3 (leave) We ＿＿ in the morning.
4 (arrive) The machines ＿＿ later this week.
5 (operate) Dr. Tompkins ＿＿ Tuesday morning.
6 (read) I ＿＿ the reports tonight.
7 (take) They ＿＿ x rays later this afternoon.
8 (open) He ＿＿ a checking account next month.
9 (tip) I ＿＿ the guide at the end of the tour.
10 (hear) You ＿＿ the orchestra in a moment.

B Follow the model.

> Ms. Kerr is going to arrive tomorrow. →
> Ms. Kerr will arrive tomorrow.

1 Lawrence is going to leave this afternoon.
2 The boss is going to order another machine.
3 Margaret is going to walk home.
4 They are going to use the car tonight.
5 Ann and I are going to arrive at noon.
6 You and Tom are going to bring the sandwiches.
7 The children are going to eat early tonight.
8 Mr. Gordon is going to explain everything tomorrow.

The future tense: interrogative forms

A **Repeat.**
Will you return soon?
Will I see you tomorrow?
Will Miss Baker see the report?

B **Practice. Follow the models.**

> Sara will finish soon. →
> Will Sara finish soon?
>
> I will be on time. →
> Will you be on time?

Mr. Davis will leave tomorrow.
Mrs. Heller will travel by train.
The children will want more dessert.
I will call the bank this afternoon.
You will need another suitcase.
We will see Helen there.

C   Repeat.

Where will he go?
What will Mrs. Sanders do?
When will she leave?

D   Follow the model.

I know where he will stay. →
Where will he stay?

I know where she will fly.
I know where the children will play.
I know when the doctor will be free.
I know when the game will begin.
I know what we will need.
I know what the teacher will say.

SUMMARY

Ann will drive home tomorrow.
Will Ann drive home tomorrow?
Where will Ann drive tomorrow?

The packages will arrive soon.
Will the packages arrive soon?
When will the packages arrive?

Will you call me tonight?
What will the travel agent do?
Who will plan the tour?

Taking off

A Complete the sentences with the future tense form of the verbs.

1 (go) _____ they _____ overseas?
2 (begin) _____ the tour _____ on time?
3 (be) _____ the weather _____ nice tomorrow?
4 (prefer) Where _____ Miss Allen _____ to go?
5 (read) _____ you _____ the brochures?
6 (enjoy) _____ everyone _____ the program?

B Write questions. Follow the model.

The tour will begin *tomorrow morning*. →
When will the tour begin?

1 Mr. Crane will need *another suit*.
2 The Logans will send *the pictures*.
3 I will return *this afternoon*.
4 *The doctor* will take care of the child.
5 *The children* will learn the rules.
6 The team will play *in the new stadium*.

Contractions of *will*

A Repeat.
She'll start her vacation tomorrow.
He'll return in a few days.
I'll write the report today.
You'll need more clothes.
We'll see you next week.
They'll take the package tour.

B Answer. Follow the model.

Will Mrs. Smith keep the pictures? →
Yes, she'll keep the pictures.

Will Miss Carroll need a passport?
Will she fill out an application?
Will Mr. Clay go sight-seeing?
Will he see the mountains?
Will you call the porter?
Will I pay in advance?
Will we eat together?
Will the Moores join a tour group?
Will they take their children?

C   Repeat.
It will be crowded.
It'll be crowded.
It'll snow tonight.

D   Answer. Use *it'll*.
Will the tour begin soon?
Will the brochure explain everything?
Will the luggage fit in the trunk?
Will it snow tonight?
Will it be nice tomorrow?
Will it be hot at the beach?

SUMMARY

will → ~~will~~ = 'll

He		He'll
She		She'll
It		It'll
I	+ 'll =	I'll
We		We'll
You		You'll
They		They'll

I will take care of the tickets.
I'll take care of the tickets.

Writing Practice

Answer the questions. Use contractions. Follow the model.

> When will the guides return? *tomorrow* →
> They'll return tomorrow.

1   What will we see? *a foreign country*
2   Where will Mr. Drake meet you? *at the agency*
3   How will you travel? *by plane*
4   Who will tip the waiter? *you*
5   When will it snow? *tonight*
6   Where will she get off? *at the next stop*
7   What will the tourists do on the island? *rest*
8   What will it cost? *a lot*

VERB PRACTICE

to look over something
to look it over

to let someone know
to let him/her know

to take care of something (someone)
to take care of it (her/him)

A Answer.

Did Miss Robbins look over the report?
Did she look it over?
Did the Meltons look over the brochures?
Did they look them over?
Did you look over the magazine?
Did you look it over?

Did you let Sara know you're coming?
Did you let her know you're coming?
Will you let me know the place and time?
Will you let me know by tomorrow?
Did Jane let Walter know the news?
Did she let him know everything?

Will someone take care of the luggage?
Will someone take care of it?
Can you take care of this for me?
Can the farmer take care of the horses for us?
Can he take care of them tomorrow, too?
Will the Halls take care of the children?
Will they take care of them for three days?

B Follow the models.

We'll take care of the suitcases. →
We'll take care of them.

I'll look over the travel plans. →
I'll look them over.

I'll look over the farm.
I'll take care of the tourists.
We'll let Mr. Hilton know.
She'll look over the correspondence.
You'll take care of the car.
I'll let the students know.

82

CONVERSATION

At the travel agency

Agent Good morning, sir. Can I help you?

Mr. Drew Yes, I'd like to take a trip on my vacation next month, but I don't know where to go.

Agent Well, what do you like to do on vacation? Do you like to go sightseeing, or do you prefer to relax on a beach somewhere?

Mr. Drew I think this year I'll just relax. I need a rest from work.

Agent I have a number of package tours to tropical islands. I'll give you some brochures and a price list. Why don't you look them over and let me know what you decide.

Mr. Drew Fine. I'll come back tomorrow then. Thank you very much.

Agent You're welcome. Good-bye.

Questions

1 Where is Mr. Drew?
2 What is he thinking of doing?
3 When is his vacation going to be?
4 Does he know where to go?
5 What does he want to do on vacation this year?
6 What does he need?
7 Does the travel agent have package tours?
8 What will the travel agent give Mr. Drew?
9 When will Mr. Drew come back?

Personal Questions

1 Do you like to travel?
2 Do you use a travel agency when you travel?
3 Will you go away on vacation this year?
4 Where will you go?
5 How will you travel—by plane, train, boat, bus, or car?
6 Do you like package tours?
7 Do you like to look at travel brochures?
8 What do you like to do on vacation?

READING

Traveling with a tour group

John and Margaret Gardner are very excited. Tonight they will be on a plane. Tonight they will begin an overseas trip.

The Gardners bought their tickets for the trip months ago. Since they are both teachers, they joined a teachers' tour group. Tickets for group flights are cheaper than tickets for regular flights, but there are usually some special rules for group flights. For a group flight, you have to buy tickets in advance. Everyone in the group leaves on the same flight, stays at the same hotels, and then returns together on the same flight.

The Gardners like the fact that the tickets were cheaper, but they had other reasons for joining a tour group. Mrs. Gardner says, "This is our first trip out of the country. We don't know where to stay, we don't know what to see. With a group there's no problem. The tour directors know all the places. They'll put us in good hotels. They'll take care of our luggage and tip the porters and maids. They'll have buses to take us to and from the airports. We'll take bus tours in each city, too."

Mr. Gardner likes the group for other reasons: "I don't know any foreign languages. I don't know anybody overseas. I don't know how much things cost. With the group I'll have people to talk to. The other people in the group are in my own profession, so we'll have similar interests. The tour directors will take us to all the interesting places and pay the bills. It will be easier for us."

Mrs. Gardner adds, "The only thing we did was get our passports and pay the travel agency. This will be a complete package tour. Everything is included: round-trip air fare, travel to and from the airports, hotels, tours in each city, tips, even breakfast and dinner. We'll pay for lunch on the trip, but that's all."

"Just think, Margaret. Tomorrow at this time we'll be in another country. We'll have dinner in a foreign city. We'll hear a strange language. I can't wait."

Questions
1 Are the Gardners excited?
2 Where will they be tonight?
3 What will they begin tonight?

4   When did they buy their tickets?
5   What did they join?
6   Were the tickets expensive?
7   What kind of tickets are expensive?
8   Are there special rules for group flights?
9   Will everyone leave on different flights?
10 Where will everyone stay?
11 Is it harder to travel with a group?
12 Is this the Gardner's first trip out of the country?
13 What will the tour directors do?
14 What kind of tours will the Gardners take in each city?
15 Does Mr. Gardner know any foreign languages?
16 Are the other people in the group teachers?
17 Who will take the Gardners to interesting places?
18 What did the Gardners have to get?
19 What is included in the tour package?
20 What will the Gardners have to pay for on the trip?
21 Where will the Gardners be tomorrow?
22 What will they do?

LESSON REVIEW

I   Complete the sentences.

passport	reason	together	relax	join
similar	rules	included	either	in advance

1   He says he needs the money. That's his _____ for working hard.
2   You're going to Bakersfield? I'm going, too. We can go _____.
3   Everything is _____ in the price of the meal: soup, meat, vegetables, dessert, and coffee.
4   Will you _____ our tour group?
5   You can't travel overseas without a _____.
6   We can pay for our tickets on the train. We don't have to buy them _____.
7   Our jobs aren't the same, but they are _____.
8   What are the _____ for traveling with a tour group?
9   You did a lot of work today. Now you can _____.
10 Paul doesn't like meat, and Helen doesn't like it _____.

II   Change from the past to the future. Follow the model.

     He went to school yesterday. →
     He will go to school again tomorrow.

1   They saw him yesterday.
2   We heard the music yesterday.
3   I answered the phone yesterday.

4 She drove to the agency yesterday.
5 The Robinsons met us yesterday.
6 It rained yesterday.
7 Edward and I helped them yesterday.
8 The travel agent called yesterday.
9 You and Fred worked until seven yesterday.
10 The dentist left at five yesterday.

III Write questions. Follow the model.

Mrs. Florham will write the report. *When* →
When will Mrs. Florham write the report?

1 The Gardners will travel on their vacation. *Where*
2 The children will play. *What*
3 The packages will arrive. *When*
4 Miss Smith will find them. *How*
5 I will prepare dinner. *When*
6 The tourists will meet the guide. *Where*

IV Answer the questions. Use contractions. Follow the model.

Will Bob go? →
Yes, he'll go.

1 Will you and Joe buy it?
2 Will they prepare dinner?
3 Will I go too?
4 Will Virginia understand?
5 Will you eat early?
6 Will the plane land soon?

V Answer the questions. Tell a story.

Will you take a trip next year?
Will you take an overseas trip?
Will you go on a group flight?
Will you all have to travel together?
Will you all stay at the same hotels?
Are all the people in the group in the same profession?
Will the tour directors pay all the bills?
Will the tour directors take everyone to interesting places?
Will the group take bus tours of the cities?
Is the group fare cheaper than the regular fare?
Will you enjoy your trip?

LESSON 5

NEW WORDS

1 Richard and Martha are
   engaged.
   They are going to be married.
   They're inviting their friends to
   the wedding.
   After the wedding, they will
   spend their honeymoon in
   Paris.
   Paris is the capital of France.

2   The real estate agent is
        showing Richard and Martha
        an apartment.
    The apartment has a lot of
        closets.
    There's a lovely view from the
        terrace.
    The apartment is available now.
    Richard and Martha can afford
        the apartment.
    The rent isn't too high.

3   Richard and Martha are reading
        the lease for the apartment.
    They have to pay a two-month
        deposit.
    The rent includes utilities:
        electricity, gas, and water.
    Will they take the apartment or
        won't they?
    They have to make a decision.

| *downtown* | the part of a city that has offices, stores, and businesses |
| | Every day Miss Lyons takes the subway to her job downtown. |

downtown
the part of a city that has offices, stores, and businesses
Every day Miss Lyons takes the subway to her job downtown.

suburbs
the small towns and areas near a large city
Mr. Gray works in the city, but he lives in the suburbs.

block
in the city or town, the place between two streets
The school is six blocks from her home.

to get used to
to know better after a time
If you're going to live in the city, you have to get used to the noise.

to hate
not to like
Donald never drinks coffee. He hates it.

reasonable
thinking well
My boss wants me to do the work of two people. He's not being reasonable.

close to
near
We want to live close to the office.

a couple of
two
I'd like to go on vacation for a couple of weeks, but I'm very busy.

enormously
very
I can't buy that car—it's enormously expensive.

A Answer the questions.

1 Who is engaged to be married?
2 Who are they inviting to the wedding?
3 Where will they spend their honeymoon?
4 What is the capital of France?
5 Who is showing Richard and Martha an apartment?
6 Does the apartment have closets?
7 Is there a nice view from the terrace?
8 Is the apartment available?
9 Can Richard and Martha afford it?
10 What are Richard and Martha reading?
11 What do they have to pay?
12 What does the rent include?
13 What do Richard and Martha have to make?
14 Does this bus go downtown?
15 Can you take a train to the suburbs?
16 How many blocks from the school do you live?
17 Are you getting used to English?
18 Do you hate coffee?
19 Are you always reasonable?

B Rewrite the sentences. Change the words in italics to a word or expression that means the same.

1 Does the rent include *gas, electricity, and water?*
2 Which bus goes *to the center of the city?*
3 Do you live *near* the hospital?
4 Please bring me *a couple of* aspirins.
5 Tom and Barbara are *going to be married.*
6 The rent is *expensive.*
7 You have to *decide* soon.

In the suburbs

STRUCTURE

Negation of the future tense

Not

A Repeat.
I will not read the newspaper today.
Sarah will not take an aspirin for her headache.
They will not go back to Mexico this winter.

B Answer. Use *no*.
Will you return tomorrow?
Will the children play this afternoon?
Will Carol and Philip read the lease?
Will we receive more mail?
Will I see you soon?
Will you and Diane visit us?

A quiet street

Ever **and** *never*

A   Repeat.
Will Tom ever return?
No, he will never return.
Will I ever finish this?
No, you'll never finish this.

B   Answer. Use *no* **and** *never*. **Follow the model.**

Will Miss Lyons ever fly again? →
No, she'll never fly again.

Will Miss Lewis ever change jobs?
Will the team ever win?
Will the teacher ever understand?
Will that car ever run again?
Will the Todds ever move to the country?
Will you ever visit Paris?
Will you ever get used to English?

SUMMARY

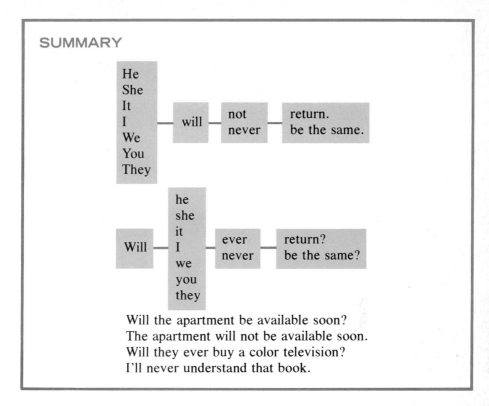

Will the apartment be available soon?
The apartment will not be available soon.
Will they ever buy a color television?
I'll never understand that book.

Writing Practice

A Follow the model.

> Many will understand. *Tom* →
> Tom will not understand.

1 The Hamilton team will win. *the Newtown team*
2 Some students will study. *other students*
3 Rose and Harry will bring the children. *Jane and Leroy*
4 The doctors will see the reports. *the nurses*
5 I will get to the capital tonight. *you*

B Follow the model.

> Will the teacher return the books? →
> Will the teacher ever return the books?
> No, he'll (she'll) never return the books.

1 Will the Kents go back to that restaurant?
2 Will the children make a decision?
3 Will Mr. Larson call again?
4 Will you take a local train?
5 Will the players learn the rules?

Contraction *won't*

A   Repeat.
He will not be on time.
He won't be on time.
Miss Lundy will not enjoy that program.
Miss Lundy won't enjoy that program.

B   Practice. Change *will not* to *won't*.
The Eliots will not come back.
I will not call her.
Sam will not pay the bill.
Miss Andrews will not sell her car.
The rent will not include utilities.
My boss will not like this report.

C   Answer. Use *no* and *won't*.
Will Sara play tomorrow?
Will you hire Mr. Hicks?
Will you and Laura rent a car?
Will I receive the check today?
Will they use the new machine?
Will the travel agents pay the porters?
Will the office be available soon?

SUMMARY

will not = won't

I will not leave a deposit. = I won't leave a deposit.
They will not be here. = They won't be here.

Writing Practice

Change the sentences from affirmative to negative. Follow the model.

He will return. →
He won't return.

1   They will prepare the reports.
2   We will write to them.
3   I will rent that apartment.
4   Sam will come back soon.
5   Mr. Jones will see us tomorrow.
6   He will wear warm clothes.
7   You will like this restaurant.
8   The team will play next Monday.

Tag endings with *won't* and *will*

Won't

A   Repeat.
He will return, won't he?
Alice will visit us, won't she?
Bob and Lou will play, won't they?
You and I will win, won't we?
It will rain, won't it?
I'll need an umbrella, won't I?
You'll read the lease, won't you?

B   Add the tag endings. Follow the model.

John will go, →
John will go, won't he?

Mary will buy the house,
I will understand,
It will be cold,
Mr. Greer will arrive soon,
You will visit us,
The Langs will arrive tomorrow,
John and I will find the place,
Mrs. Davis will explain,

Will

A   Repeat.
They won't pay, will they?
Tom won't sign, will he?
Susan won't study, will she?
Walter and I won't enjoy it, will we?
It won't snow, will it?
You won't leave yet, will you?
I won't hate the city, will I?

A house in the suburbs

B   Add the tag endings. Follow the model.

John won't go, →
John won't go, will he?

We won't see you,
Susan won't swim,
I won't have to work,
You won't join the group,
Barbara and I won't need money,
Ralph won't fill the tank,
The children won't go to school Saturday,
It won't be available soon,

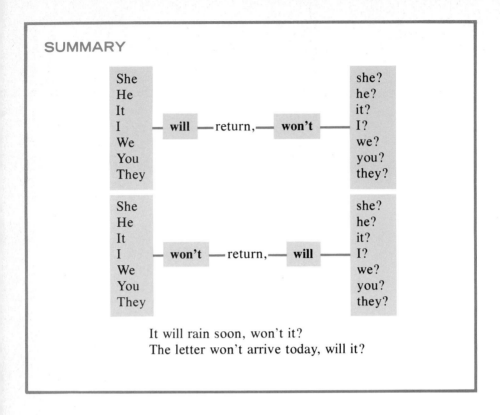

It will rain soon, won't it?
The letter won't arrive today, will it?

Writing Practice

Add the correct tag endings.

1 The secretaries will work Thursday, _____?
2 Ms. Glover will hire a new secretary, _____?
3 The tour director will tip the maids, _____?
4 You won't order more food, _____?
5 Daniel won't know the place, _____?
6 I will like the museum, _____?
7 Harold and Marjorie won't buy the building, _____?
8 You and I won't need a taxi, _____?
9 It won't snow this week, _____?
10 You and Henry will wait for us, _____?

Ordinal numbers to *25th*

A   Repeat.
This is the first floor.
This is the second floor.
This is the third floor.

B Substitute.

This is the

| first |
| second |
| third |
| fourth |
| fifth |
| sixth |

floor.

We live in the

| seventh |
| eighth |
| ninth |
| tenth |

house on the left.

They pay us on the

| first |
| fifth |
| tenth |

of the month.

C Answer. Follow the model.

What floor, please?   (one) →
First please.

What floor, please?   (three)
What floor, please?   (five)
What floor, please?   (eight)
What floor, please?   (ten)

D Repeat.

Today is the eleventh.
Tomorrow is the twelfth.
Today is the thirteenth.
Tomorrow is the fourteenth.

E Substitute.

The appointment is for December

| fifteenth. |
| sixteenth. |
| seventeenth. |
| eighteenth. |
| nineteenth. |

Their office is on the

| twentieth |
| twenty-first |
| twenty-second |
| twenty-third |
| twenty-fourth |
| twenty-fifth |

floor.

F   Answer. Follow the models.

Is your apartment on the first floor? →
No, it's on the second.

Is your office on the nineteenth floor? →
No, it's on the twentieth.

Is your apartment on the fifteenth floor?
Is your office on the twenty-fourth floor?
Is your apartment on the third floor?
Is your office on the ninth floor?
Is your apartment on the second floor?
Is your office on the seventeenth floor?
Is your apartment on the fifth floor?
Is your office on the tenth floor?

SUMMARY

1	one	first	14	fourteen	fourteenth
2	two	second	15	fifteen	fifteenth
3	three	third	16	sixteen	sixteenth
4	four	fourth	17	seventeen	seventeenth
5	five	fifth	18	eighteen	eighteenth
6	six	sixth	19	nineteen	nineteenth
7	seven	seventh	20	twenty	twentieth
8	eight	eighth	21	twenty-one	twenty-first
9	nine	ninth	22	twenty-two	twenty-second
10	ten	tenth	23	twenty-three	twenty-third
11	eleven	eleventh	24	twenty-four	twenty-fourth
12	twelve	twelfth	25	twenty-five	twenty-fifth
13	thirteen	thirteenth			

There are three houses on this block.
I live in the third house.

Writing Practice

Write the ordinal number that goes with the cardinal number. Follow the model.

  six →
  sixth

1 one
2 seven
3 nine
4 twenty-two
5 eleven
6 three
7 seventeen
8 twelve
9 two
10 eight
11 twenty-five
12 nineteen
13 five
14 fourteen
15 four

VERB PRACTICE

to pay
to pay for

Answer.
Do you pay the bills once a month?
Did Mrs. Tyler pay the hospital bills?
Did she pay the water bill?
Did Mr. Warner pay the rent?
Does he pay the rent on the fifteenth?

Did we pay the dentist last night?
Do you pay the doctor after each visit?
Does that company pay the secretaries a lot?
Did everyone pay the travel agent?
Do I pay the waitress or the cashier?

Did Millie pay for her bicycle?
Did she pay a lot for it?
Do I have to pay for water?
Does the agent pay for everything?
Can I pay for the sweater by check?

READING

House or apartment?

Frank Whitney and Doris Morgan are engaged to be married. They have many decisions to make: how many people they will invite to the wedding, where they will spend their honeymoon, and—most important of all—where they will live.

Doris and Frank are both lawyers. They plan to move to the capital and open an office there together. It wasn't hard to find an office, but where will they look for a home?

"Look, Doris. I will *not* live downtown. I'm not used to apartments. I *hate* apartments, and I won't live in one. I'm a country boy—I hate the city."

"I know how you feel, Frank, but be reasonable. You want a house, but you also want to live close to the office. You know we can't afford a house in the city—they're all too expensive. We *can* afford a house in the suburbs or the country, but we won't want to spend two or three hours a day on the train, will we? So what do we do?"

"I don't know, Doris. Apartments are so small. I know I'll never get used to one."

"They're not *all* small."

"Most of them are. We'll want a couple of bedrooms, a big living room, a dining room, a nice kitchen. You won't find all that in an apartment, will you?"

"Frank, we'll never find a perfect place, will we? But there are some nice apartments. Listen, the real estate people called today. They have an apartment on K Street. K Street, Frank! That's two blocks from the office! We can walk to work."

"What's it like—a closet?"

"Not at all. It has two bedrooms (one's a little small, but that's all right), two bathrooms, a living room, dining room, kitchen, and a terrace. It'll be available in July. What do you think?"

"I think it sounds enormously expensive."

"Well, the rent is a little high, but it includes utilities. We won't have to pay for electricity, gas, or water. They want a two-month deposit. The lease is for two years. Frank, it's on the seventeenth floor! I'm sure the view from the terrace will be lovely."

"Seventeenth floor! I hope there's an elevator."

Questions

1. Are Doris and Frank going to be married?
2. Do they have to make some decisions?
3. What is the most important decision they have to make?
4. Where are Doris and Frank going to open an office?
5. Was it hard to find an office?
6. Does Frank want to live downtown?
7. Does he like apartments?
8. Does he like the city?
9. Does Doris understand how Frank feels?
10. Can Doris and Frank afford a house in the city?
11. Where can they afford a house?
12. Will they want to spend a lot of time on the train?
13. How many rooms will they want?
14. Will they ever find a perfect place?
15. Where do the real estate people have an apartment?
16. When will the apartment be available?
17. Does Frank think it sounds expensive?
18. Is the rent low or high?
19. Does it include utilities?
20. For how many years is the lease?
21. What floor is the apartment on?
22. Will the view from the terrace be nice?

Personal Questions

1. Do you own your own home or do you rent it?
2. Is your home an apartment or a house?
3. What utilities does it have?
4. Is it close to school or work?
5. How do you get to work from your home?
6. Which do you prefer, a house or an apartment? Why?

LESSON REVIEW

I   Complete the sentences.

1. The rent includes _____: gas, water, and electricity.
2. Jane Logan has to decide where to live. She has to make a _____.
3. The rent isn't low—it's _____.
4. Tokyo is the _____ of Japan.
5. You have enough money to pay for that dress. You can _____ it.
6. The airport is near the city. It's _____ to the city.
7. That hat is very nice. It's _____.
8. You want to go to the center of the city? This bus goes _____.
9. Tom and Laura are going to be husband and wife. They are going to be _____.
10. Miss Sanders has two magazines. She has a _____ of magazines.

II Complete the sentences. Use *not* or *never*.

   1 Will they ever return?
     No, they will _____ return.
   2 Will Sam find the copies?
     No, he will _____ find them.
   3 Will Bob and Sandra work tonight?
     No, they will _____ work tonight.
   4 Will you and Tim ever move to the city?
     No, we will _____ move to the city.
   5 Will the Johnsons ever live in an apartment?
     No, they will _____ live in an apartment.
   6 Will I receive the copies today?
     No, you will _____ receive them today.
   7 Will Ellen ever learn English?
     No, she will _____learn English.
   8 Will you and Phil eat at home tonight?
     No, we will _____ eat at home tonight.

III Complete the questions with the correct tag endings.

   1 The plane will arrive on time, _____?
   2 You won't work tonight, _____?
   3 The doctor and nurse will work together, _____?
   4 Mrs. Foster will take her medicine, _____?
   5 I won't need help, _____?
   6 You'll go to the real estate office, _____?
   7 Gilbert won't take the bus, _____?
   8 It won't be too cold, _____?
   9 Mrs. Edgar will leave a deposit, _____?
  10 Mr. Grant will see you tonight, _____?

IV Answer the questions. Tell a story.

Will the Grahams move to the capital?
Will they move there next year?
Are the Grahams lawyers?
Will their office be downtown?
Will they live in the country or the suburbs?
Will they live in a house or an apartment?
Will the apartment have a terrace?
Will the rent be high or low?
Will they walk to work?
Will they like their new apartment?
Will they be happy there?

LESSON 6

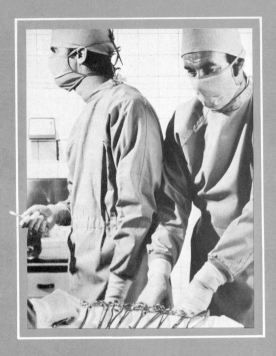

NEW WORDS

1   Chemistry isn't difficult for
      Kathy.
    Her ambition is to become a
      chemist.
    She wants to enter the field of
      chemistry.

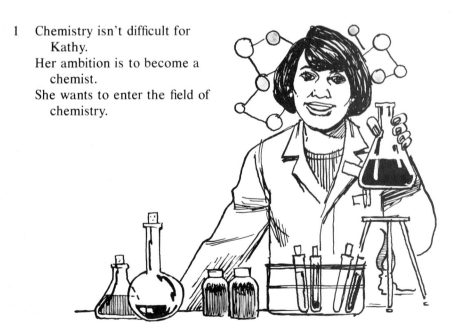

2   John is studying mathematics.
     He wants a career as a
        computer programmer.
     Computers are common in
        business.
     Most large companies use
        them.

3   Jane is a teenager.
     She is registering with an
        employment agency.
     She wants to work part-time
        after school.
     She has a short résumé.
     Her job experience is limited.
     She has only one former
        employer.

4   The Blank Company is opening
      a branch office here.
    They have a want ad in the
      local paper.
    They are looking for people
      with talent.
    There are a lot of job openings.
    The list goes on and on.
    There is a wide choice of jobs.

medicine	what doctors study; the profession of doctors Richard wants to be a doctor. He is going to study medicine.
medical	about medicine We always need more people in the medical profession.
bookkeeping	what bookkeepers do I studied bookkeeping for two years.
to exist	to be Airplanes didn't exist a hundred years ago.
to run into	to meet, to find suddenly The tour group ran into several problems: bad weather, late flights, lost reservations.
to set up	to plan Miss Comstock and Mr. Harris want to see Mr. Jones tomorrow morning. Please set up the appointments. *Past tense:* Mr. Temple set up the meeting yesterday.

financial   about money

Mr. and Mrs. Landings are rich. They don't have any financial problems.

outside   not in

Today many women also work outside the home.

shortly   soon

The doctor is busy now, but he will see you shortly.

A   Answer the questions.

1   Is chemistry difficult for Kathy?
2   What is Kathy's ambition?
3   What field does she want to enter?
4   What is John studying?
5   Who wants a career as a computer programmer?
6   Are computers common in business?
7   Who uses them?
8   What is Jane?
9   Is she registering with an employment agency?
10   When does she want to work?
11   Is her résumé short or long?
12   How many former employers does she have?
13   What is the Blank Company opening?
14   What do they have in the local paper?
15   What kind of people are they looking for?
16   Are there a lot of job openings?
17   Is there a wide choice of jobs?
18   Do we need more people in the medical field?
19   Did airplanes exist a hundred years ago?
20   Did the pilot run into bad weather?
21   Can the secretary set up the appointments?
22   Do most people have financial problems sometimes?

B   Ask questions. Use *what kind of.*

She's looking for a *fancy* dress. →
What kind of dress is she looking for?

Bill has *medical* problems. →
What kind of problems does Bill have?

1   Miss Templeton wants a *part-time* job.
2   The Bakers own an *employment* agency.
3   Mrs. Andrews is writing a *financial* report.
4   Mr. Slade wants to make a *person-to-person* call.
5   Aruba is a *tropical* island.
6   Sandra watches *cultural* programs on television.

MORE NEW WORDS

knife

leaf

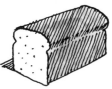

loaf of bread

tree

STRUCTURE

Gerunds

A   Repeat.
Typing is easy for Bob.
I think cooking is boring.
Reading is always popular.

B   Answer.
Is speaking English difficult?
Is reading interesting?
Is teaching exciting?
Is writing letters easy for Ann?
Is traveling alone hard for Tom?
Is tipping sometimes hard for tourists?
Is choosing a career important?
Is saving money difficult for some people?
Is typing boring?

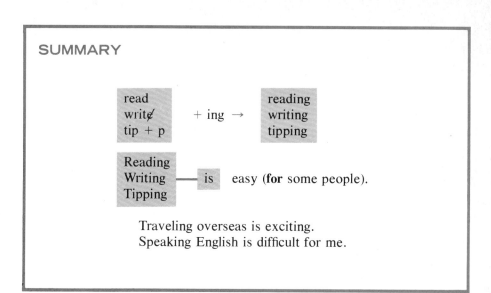

SUMMARY

read
write + ing → reading
writing
tip + p → tipping

Reading
Writing — is easy (**for** some people).
Tipping

Traveling overseas is exciting.
Speaking English is difficult for me.

Writing Practice

Follow the model.

> Mrs. Martin likes to teach. →
> Teaching is easy for her.

1 Miss Nelson likes to read.
2 Mr. Harris likes to play golf.
3 Mrs. Travis likes to write letters.
4 Bill likes to type.
5 Laura likes to speak English.
6 Mr. and Mrs. White like to cook.
7 Jane and Tom like to take pictures.
8 Miss Blake likes to drive.

Impersonal expressions with *it*

A Repeat.
It's easy to cook vegetables.
It's hard for me to play tennis.
It's important to work hard.

B Answer.
Is it hard to learn languages?
Is it difficult to choose a career?
Is it nice to have talent?
Is it important to register with an agency?
Is it time to look for a job?
Is it exciting to go on vacation?
Is it boring to type all day long?
Is it too late to catch the train?
Is it easy for Sara to speak English?
Is it hard for her to teach it?

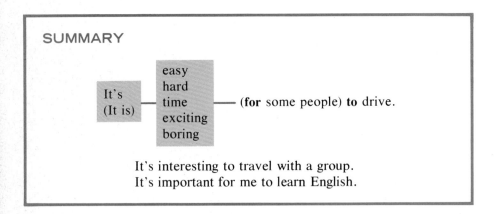

SUMMARY

| It's (It is) | easy / hard / time / exciting / boring | (for some people) to drive. |

It's interesting to travel with a group.
It's important for me to learn English.

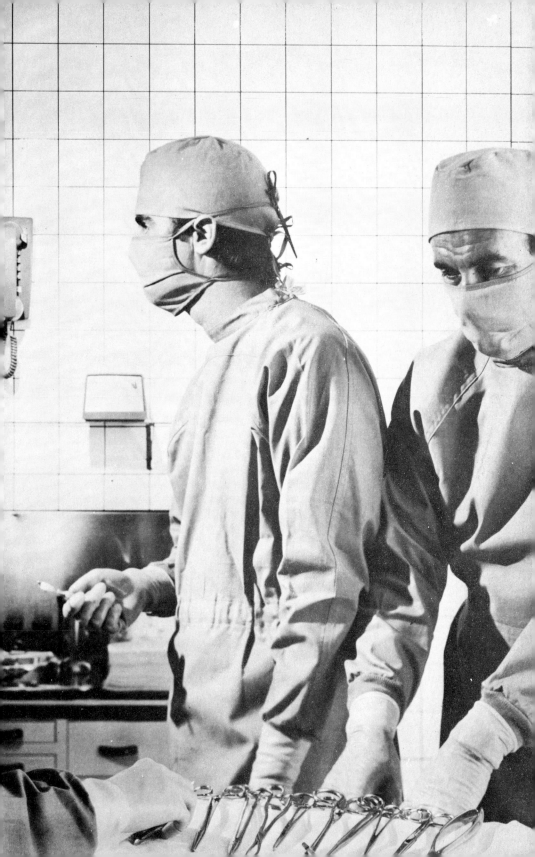

Writing Practice

Follow the models.

> hard / type fast →
> It's hard to type fast.
>
> easy / Harry / type →
> It's easy for Harry to type.

1 important / study
2 time / unpack
3 safe / go in the water
4 easy / Miss Andrews / learn chemistry
5 too late / go out
6 better / wait for the train
7 difficult / some people / choose a career
8 hard / Tom / answer in English

A teacher

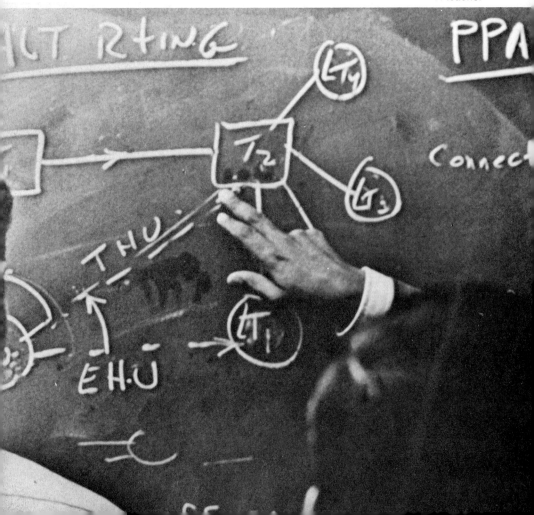

Irregular noun plurals: $f \rightarrow v$

A **Repeat.**

The knife is on the table.
The knives are on the table.

The child has a loaf of bread.
The child has two loaves of bread.

The shelf is too high.
The shelves are too high.

B **Answer.**

Does the waiter need more knives?
Does Mrs. Park know the other wives?
Do police officers save lives?
Do the leaves fall from the trees?
Does Mr. Fleming need three loaves of bread?
Does Betty like the new shelves?

li̶f̶e̶		lives
kni̶f̶e̶	+ ves →	knives
wi̶f̶e̶		wives

lea̶f̶		leaves
loa̶f̶	+ ves →	loaves
shel̶f̶		shelves

Doctors and nurses save lives every day.
Ann needs more shelves for her books.

Writing Practice

Make the words plural.

1 (leaf)   That tree has no _____.
2 (wife)   The _____ are waiting for their husbands.
3 (loaf)   Please buy two _____ of bread.
4 (shelf)   The _____ are too high for the child.
5 (life)   They saved many _____ during the storm.
6 (knife)   There are no _____ in the drawer.

Prepositions *before* and *after*

A   Repeat.
John will arrive before one o'clock.
They want to leave before Tuesday.

I left after midnight.
The Wilsons arrived after dinner.

B   Answer.
Can Joe leave before six o'clock?
Can you deliver the checks before noon?
Can they have dinner before seven o'clock?
Can they finish the work before the end of the week?
Can you wash the car before lunch?
Did the package arrive after breakfast?
Did it snow after the twenty-fifth?
Did you work after school?
Did the Larsons travel after their wedding?
Did you have an appointment after lunch?

SUMMARY

before noon   after the fourteenth

Laura left at eleven-thirty. She left before midnight.
Tom had breakfast. Then he washed the car. He washed the car after breakfast.

Writing Practice

Complete the sentences. Use *before* or *after*.

1   Susan has breakfast. Then she opens the mail. She opens the mail _____ breakfast.
2   Tom arrived in the morning. He arrived _____ noon.
3   Doris goes to school. Then she goes to work. She works _____ school.
4   The Bradleys went on a honeymoon. Then they visited the Smiths. The Bradleys visited the Smiths _____ their honeymoon.
5   Bill typed the letters. Then he had lunch. He typed the letters _____ lunch.
6   The children had dinner. Then they watched television. They watched television _____ dinner.

VERB PRACTICE

to run into something (someone)
to run into it (her/him)

to get used to something
to get used to it

to bring something in
to bring in something
to bring it in

to type something up
to type up something
to type it up

to set something up
to set up something
to set it up

Office workers

A **Answer.**

Did you run into Mary in the city?
Did you run into her in the store?
Did Harry run into trouble with the car?
Did the Bakers run into financial problems?

Did Mrs. Moore get used to the noise in the city?
Did she get used to it fast?
Did she get used to the traffic?
Did Mr. Moore get used to it, too?

Did Mr. Phillips type up the list?
Did he type it up in the office?
Can you type this up for me?
Can you type it up before noon?

Did Mrs. Lane bring in the correspondence files?
Did she bring them in this morning?
Can you bring in your résumé?
Can you bring it in next week?

Will Paul set up the appointments?
Will he set them up for tomorrow afternoon?
Did Laura set up the interview?
Did she set it up for nine o'clock?

B Follow the model.

> Please type up the report. →
> Please type it up.

Please type up the résumé.
Please bring in the Pearson file.
Please set up the meetings.
Please bring in the newspapers.
Please type up the financial reports.
Please set up the interviews.

CONVERSATION

At the employment agency

Receptionist	Good morning, sir. Can I help you?
Mr. Stone	Yes, I'd like to register with your agency.
Receptionist	All right. Someone will see you shortly. Please fill out this form while you're waiting.
	(*Later*)
Mrs. Todd	Mr. Stone, why did you leave your last job?
Mr. Stone	I worked in a branch office of the Blank Company. They ran into financial troubles and had to close the office.
Mrs. Todd	I see on your application that you have fifteen years' experience as a bookkeeper. Can you get references from your former employer?
Mr. Stone	Oh, yes. I'm sure they'll give me references. One thing I don't have, though, is a résumé. I wasn't sure how to write it.
Mrs. Todd	Here. You can use this one as a model. After you type yours up, bring it in and we'll make copies of it. I'm sure we'll find a good job for you. There are several openings in bookkeeping right now. I'll set up some interviews and call you Wednesday.
Mr. Stone	Fine. Thank you very much.

Questions

1 Who wants to register with the employment agency?
2 What does he have to fill out?
3 Who is Mr. Stone's former employer?
4 What did the Blank Company run into?
5 How much experience does Mr. Stone have?
6 Will the Blank Company give him references?
7 Why doesn't Mr. Stone have a résumé?
8 Will the agency make copies of his résumé?
9 Are there any openings in bookkeeping now?
10 What will Mrs. Todd set up?

Personal Questions

1 The last time you looked for a job, did you go to an employment agency or to a company?
2 Who did you talk to?
3 Did you know what kind of job you wanted?
4 How many people interviewed you?
5 Do you like to go for interviews?
6 Do you know how to write a résumé?

READING

Choosing a career

A hundred years ago it was easy to choose a career. People usually did what their parents did. The farmer's son became a farmer; the dentist's son became a dentist; the banker's son became a banker. Most women became wives and mothers and didn't work outside the home. For those women who worked outside the home, the choice of jobs was limited. Teaching, nursing, and factory work were the most common jobs for women.

Today choosing a career can be very difficult. It can also be very exciting. Young women and men have a wide choice of fields to enter. There are hundreds of jobs today that didn't even exist in the last century: computer programmer, x-ray technician, pilot, truck driver . . . the list goes on and on.

It's important for young people to know what they want. They have to ask themselves, "Do I want to work with people? Do I want to work with things? What are my talents? How important is money? What kind of education will I need and how long will it take to get it?"

Sometimes people know what they want to do when they're still very young. Dr. Laura Mitchell doesn't remember when she decided to become a doctor. "It was my ambition even when I was a child," she says. As a teenager, she worked part-time in hospitals after school. She became friends with the local doctor. She knew a lot about medicine even before she started medical school. "Choosing a career wasn't a problem for me," she says. "I made that decision early."

It's never too early to choose a career. It's never too late to change careers. Mark Singleton was a chemist for thirty years. One day he thought, "This job was interesting once, but it isn't any more. It's time to do something else." Now he teaches chemistry and mathematics at the local high school. "Working with teenagers makes me feel young," he says.

A hundred years ago it was easy to choose a career. Today it's not always easy, but it's nice to have a choice.

Questions
1   Was it easy to choose a career a hundred years ago?
2   What did people usually do?
3   What did most women do?
4   Did women have a wide choice of jobs?
5   What were the most common jobs for women?
6   Is choosing a career more difficult today?
7   What are some jobs that didn't exist in the last century?
8   What do young people have to ask themselves?
9   Does Dr. Mitchell remember when she decided to become a doctor?
10   As a teenager, where did she work after school?
11   Was choosing a career a problem for her?
12   Is it ever too late to change careers?
13   What was Mark Singleton's job for thirty years?
14   What does he do now?
15   How does working with teenagers make him feel?
16   Is it nice to have a choice of careers?

LESSON REVIEW

I   Complete the sentences.

ambition	financial	talent
exist	after	former
teenager	common	opening
employer	difficult	before

1. That woman is a great artist. She has a lot of _____.
2. Most people in the office have calculators. Calculators are _____ in the office.
3. Sam is fifteen years old. He's a _____.
4. Alma watched the soccer game. Then she went home. She went home _____ the game.
5. There weren't any computers in the nineteenth century. Computers didn't _____ then.
6. One of our bookkeepers left the company. Now we have an _____ in the bookkeeping department.
7. I work for Mrs. Lawrence. She is my _____.
8. I get dressed and then I have breakfast. I get dressed _____ breakfast.
9. I'm in medical school. My _____ is to become a doctor.
10. I can't learn chemistry. It's too _____ for me.
11. That company has no money. They're having serious _____ problems.
12. Miss Prescott was my teacher five years ago. She's my _____ teacher.

II   Rewrite the sentences. Follow the model.

> It's hard for teenagers to choose a career. →
> Choosing a career is hard for teenagers.

1. It's boring to watch television all day.
2. It's difficult for Ann to read fast.
3. It's exciting to travel around the world.
4. It's important for David to speak well.
5. It's interesting to teach young children.
6. It's easy for children to learn languages.

III Write a sentence about each of the following.

1. Choosing a career
2. Going for an interview
3. Hiring people
4. Speaking English
5. Getting a good education

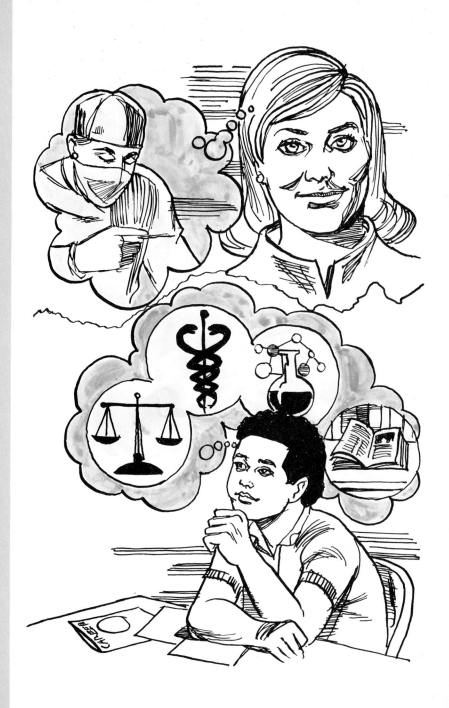

LESSON 7

NEW WORDS

1 The train is full of commuters.
   It's crossing the railroad
     bridge.
   The weather is clearing up.
   The clouds are going away.

2   The people are in a theater.
    They look happy.
    They're watching the actors
        and actresses.
    The play is a comedy.
    One member of the audience is
        sleeping.
    His eyes are closed.
    He slept the last time, too.

3   The Minister of Finance is
        talking to the Prime Minister
        in person.
    She is presenting plans for a
        tax cut.
    Will the Prime Minister
        approve the plans?

sports	games Baseball, soccer, and tennis are sports.
entrance	where people enter a building I'll meet you at eight o'clock in front of the theater entrance.
song	words and music Most teenagers like to listen to popular songs on the radio.
to defeat	to win against The Hamilton soccer team defeated the Brighton soccer team by a score of 2 to 1.
awful	very bad I don't like that song. I think it's awful.
to blame	to think badly of Paula hates her job, but you can't blame her. It's an awful job.
to stay tuned	to keep the radio on "This is radio station SPQR. Stay tuned now for the news."
I'm afraid . . .	I'm sorry, but . . . Mr. and Mrs. Hall, I'm afraid your son has to go to the hospital.
bored	how you feel when you're doing or watching something boring, or when you have nothing to do The children are bored. They have nothing to do.
until	up to the time of The Martins will stay in the city until Wednesday. Then they'll leave.

A Answer the questions.

1   Is the train full of commuters?
2   What is it crossing?
3   Is the weather clearing up?
4   Where are the people?
5   How do they look?
6   Who are they watching?
7   What kind of play is it?
8   What is one member of the audience doing?
9   Are his eyes open or closed?
10   Who is the Minister of Finance talking to?
11   What is she presenting?
12   Who can approve the plans?
13   Which sports do you like?
14   Do you listen to songs on the radio?
15   Does your team always defeat the other team?
16   Do some people get bored easily?

B Complete the sentences.

1 My wife is a _____. She goes to the city every day to work.
2 I hate modern art. I think it's _____.
3 The movie was great. The _____ loved it.
4 We can't cross the river. There's no _____.
5 Please be quiet. The children are going to _____.
6 The weather was cloudy in the morning, but it _____ up in the afternoon.
7 My uncle is a conductor. He works for the _____.
8 The Smithville baseball team _____ the Harrison team by a score of 4 to 2.

A reporter

sad

handsome

STRUCTURE

The future progressive tense

A Repeat.
I will be studying for another hour.
She will be living in the city for a few days.
They will be waiting for you.

B Substitute.

The tourists
Miss Prescott
The tour guide | will be staying for another week.
We
I

C Answer.

Will Ann be working late?
Will she be working late all week?
Will Mr. Jackson be staying here?
Will he be eating with us?
Will the children be studying tonight?
Will they be reading all evening?
Will the trains be running late tomorrow?
Will you be seeing Miss Kent in Europe?
Will I be hearing from you?

Radios

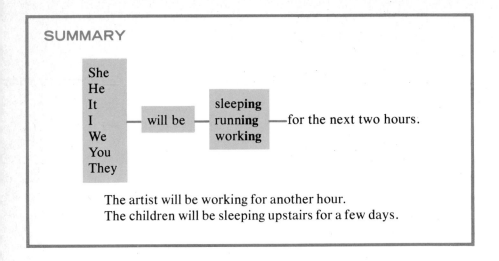

The artist will be working for another hour.
The children will be sleeping upstairs for a few days.

Writing Practice

A Complete the sentences with the future progressive form of the verbs. Follow the model.

> (study) Wanda _____ chemistry for another six months. →
> Wanda will be studying chemistry for another six months.

1 (deliver) Ann and Charles _____ packages all day tomorrow.
2 (open) The stores _____ earlier during December.
3 (hire) The HMQ Company _____ many new people next month.
4 (run) The buses _____ late this week.
5 (wait) The Petersons _____ for you.
6 (travel) You and Bill _____ a lot next year.

B Answer the questions. Use the cues.

1 What will you be doing during the summer? *working*
2 Who will be staying with you next week? *my aunt*
3 Where will you be living during medical school? *in the city*
4 How much longer will you be studying? *for another hour*
5 When will they be leaving? *in a few minutes*
6 Where will Joan be working? *on the twentieth floor*

Tag endings with *didn't* and *did*

Didn't

A Repeat.
Mrs. Layton approved the report, didn't she?
Your brother stayed with you, didn't he?

It rained a lot, didn't it?
I made a mistake, didn't I?
We needed more help, didn't we?
You liked the actors, didn't you?
The commuters had trouble, didn't they?

B **Add the tag endings.**
Ellen worked after school,
Mrs. Gordon wrote the play,
Tom played for the Hamilton team,
Mr. Miller presented the plans,
The weather cleared up,
The train left on time,
I closed my eyes,
I invited everybody,
You and I worked hard,
We wrote the best letters,
You bought a new calculator,
You went to the theater,
Your employers gave you references,
The children went to the park,

Did

A **Repeat.**
Mr. Pierce didn't finish the letter, did he?
We didn't have a good time, did we?
I didn't make enough copies, did I?
The children didn't get wet, did they?

B **Add the tag endings.**
Mr. Rogers didn't arrive on time,
He didn't take the subway,
Miss Harrison didn't call back,
She didn't write to Mr. Bell,
The play didn't start late,
The taxi didn't go very fast,
I didn't leave very late,
I didn't pack enough shirts,
You and I didn't shout,
We didn't find a taxi,
You didn't go overseas,
You didn't join a tour group,
The Andersons didn't rent a car,
They didn't use your car,

SUMMARY

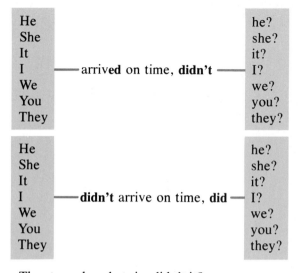

He		he?
She		she?
It		it?
I	arrived on time, **didn't**	I?
We		we?
You		you?
They		they?

He		he?
She		she?
It		it?
I	**didn't** arrive on time, **did**	I?
We		we?
You		you?
They		they?

The store closed at six, didn't it?
We didn't need the extra copies, did we?

Writing Practice

Write the correct tag endings.

1   You used a calculator, _____?
2   Ms. Glover checked the applications, _____?
3   Mr. Forbes didn't go to the office today, _____?
4   The trip didn't take long, _____?
5   I didn't take your book, _____?
6   The Bakers found a house, _____?
7   You didn't get nervous, _____?
8   You and I worked hard, _____?
9   We didn't finish on time, _____?
10   The tourists didn't make hotel reservations, _____?

A radio announcer

Double object pronouns

A **Repeat.**

Laura bought Mary the blouse.
She bought the blouse for Mary.
She bought it for her.

Laura gave Mary the blouse.
She gave the blouse to Mary.
She gave it to her.

B   Answer. Follow the model.

> Did you buy the shirt for John? →
> Yes, I bought the shirt for John.

Did Sheila buy the camera for you?
Did you make the hat for Sara?
Did Bill cook the vegetables for the children?
Did you save that seat for me?
Did Mrs. Norris get the keys for us?
Did you leave the money for the package?
Did you hand the tools to the artist?
Did Mr. Lewis give the painting to Mrs. Preston?
Did the secretary send the letter to Miss Corey?
Did you tell the joke to the English students?
Did the captain kick the ball to me?
Did she offer the cup to you?
Did you take the prescription to the pharmacist?

C   Answer. Follow the model.

> Did Laura buy it for him? →
> Yes, she bought it for him.

Did Sandra buy it for her?
Did she make them for us?
Did you leave it for him?
Did you cook it for them?
Did John get it for you?
Did he save them for me?
Did the teacher hand them to us?
Did she take them to him?
Did we send it to her?
Did you tell it to them?
Did Mr. Barrett give them to you?
Did he offer it to me?
Did I kick it to him?

D   Answer. Follow the model.

> Did Mr. Lee get the tickets for Mrs. Carroll? →
> Yes, he got them for her.

Did Mr. Clay get the brochures for Miss Stone?
Did he make the dessert for the children?
Did Mrs. Milner save the newspaper for her husband?
Did she buy the magazines for you?
Did the children cook the food for their parents?
Did you leave the files for me?
Did you give the pictures to Mrs. Borden?
Did she send the report to Pryor?
Did Mr. Brand offer the tickets to the children?
Did he tell the jokes to the members of the audience?
Did you take the copies to Mrs. Shilling?

SUMMARY

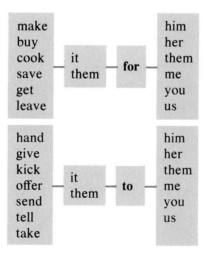

I gave Miss Parker the books.
I gave her the books.
I gave the books to Miss Parker.
I gave them to Miss Parker.
I gave them to her.

Writing Practice

A Rewrite the sentences. Follow the model.

> We cooked *the soup* for *the children.* →
> We cooked it for them.

1 I sent *the plans* to you.
2 Mrs. Kelsey bought *the shirts* for *her husband.*
3 She is going to offer *the radio* to *the children.*
4 Mr. Slager saved *the magazine* for *Laura.*
5 Did you get *the tickets* for me?
6 Tom handed *the tools* to *Mr. Nelson.*
7 Miss Hilton made *the chair* for *the boy.*
8 I told *the story* to *the students.*
9 The child took *the prescription* to *the pharmacist.*
10 They left *the money* for us.

B Complete the sentences. Use *for* or *to.*

1 We sent it _____ them.
2 I cooked them _____ you.
3 She saved it _____ us.
4 The captain kicked it _____ me.
5 Please offer them _____ her.
6 Did you make it _____ me?

Preposition *by*

A Repeat.
He is standing by the door.
I parked the car by the house.

B **Practice. Change *near* to *by*.**
The book is near the typewriter.
She is standing near the door.
We put the medicine near the bed.
The bus is near the platform.
The paper is near your chair.

C **Repeat.**
The play is by Ralph Jones.
The book is by Margaret Adams.

D **Follow the model.**

Jane Clark wrote the play. →
The play is by Jane Clark.

Sam Grover wrote the music.
Louise Lane wrote the story.
Thomas Anderson wrote the book.
Harold Johnson wrote the play.
Dolores Weaver wrote the report.

E **Repeat.**
We will be there by two o'clock.
They will arrive by Wednesday.

F **Answer.**
Will you arrive by nine o'clock?
Will they call by this evening?
Will we see you by Saturday?
Will the package get here by Thursday?
Will she finish the book by tonight?

SUMMARY

The car is *near* the entrance.
The car is *by* the entrance.

John Gerard *wrote* the book.
The book is *by* John Gerard.

The bus arrives *not later than* two o'clock.
The bus arrives by two o'clock.

A Rewrite the sentences. Change the italicized words to *by*.

    1   The plane will land *not later than* seven o'clock.
    2   We finish work *not later than* six-thirty.
    3   The calculator is *next to* the typewriter.
    4   Our seats are *next to* the orchestra.
    5   The program is over *not later than* eleven o'clock.
    6   The critic stands *next to* the door.

B Follow the model.

    Ms. Harvey wrote the book. →
    The book is by Ms. Harvey.

    1   Roy Green wrote the music.
    2   Our teacher wrote the story.
    3   Dr. Andrews wrote the report.
    4   Benson and Gray wrote the program.

VERB PRACTICE

to look + *adjective*

A **Repeat.**
The audience looks bored.
Mr. Sanders looked well.
That book looks easy.

B **Answer.**
Does Mrs. Powers look better today?
Does she look happy?
Do the children look bored?
Does one child look sad?
Did Mr. Blair look awful this morning?
Did Tim look handsome in his new suit?
Did Laura look beautiful at the wedding?
Does that book look difficult?
Does this lesson look hard?
Do those vegetables look fresh?
Does that shirt look dirty?
Does the car look clean now?

READING

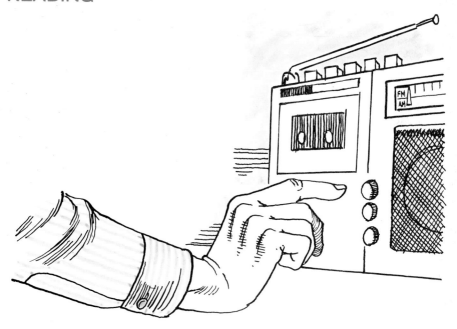

The radio news

Roger Carlin   Good evening. This is Roger Carlin with the SPQR Radio News. With me is Nancy Fulton with the local news. Nancy?

Nancy Fulton   Thank you, Roger. I'm afraid I have some bad news for commuters. The Main Avenue railroad bridge is closed. There is no train service into or out of the city. Extra buses will be running until the bridge is open. Railroad director Lawrence Bell says the bridge will be open by nine P.M. The evening rush hour didn't start very well, did it?

Roger   No, it didn't, Nancy. The capital: Minister of Finance Margaret Murton today approved plans for a tax cut. She will present the plans to the Prime Minister tomorrow morning. "I want to give them to him in person," she said. The Prime Minister will be studying the plans for the next few days.

Sports: In soccer, West City defeated North End today by a score of four to two. Gary Cresley scored two goals for West City.

Nancy   Theater: "Trouble in Trenton," a new play by Hazel Margate, opened last night at the Victoria Theater. Here is Peter Hampton with his review.

Peter Hampton   Greetings. Well, last night I saw "Trouble in Trenton." After the play I stood by the theater entrance and listened to the members of the audience. Their opinions and mine are the same. Let me give them to you. Miss Margate's new play is awful. She calls it a comedy, but there's nothing funny in it. The actors and actresses look bored, and you can't blame them. The play is boring. If you want to sleep for three hours, go see this play.

Nancy   Peter tells people what he thinks, doesn't he?

Roger   Yes, indeed. Now, what about tomorrow's weather, Nancy?

Nancy   We're going to have showers and cool temperatures tomorrow. Temperatures will be dropping for the next few days, but the clouds will clear up by tomorrow night.

Roger   Thanks, Nancy. Stay tuned now for the Chuck Chambers show with the latest popular songs. Until tomorrow evening, good night from the SPQR Radio News.

Questions

1 Who is speaking?
2 Who is going to give the local news?
3 Does she have some bad news for commuters?
4 Which bridge is closed?
5 Is there any train service into or out of the city?
6 How long will extra buses be running?
7 When will the bridge be open?
8 Did the rush hour start well?
9 Who approved plans for a tax cut?
10 When will she present the plans to the Prime Minister?
11 Does she want to give them to him in person?
12 Will he be studying them for the next few days?
13 Who defeated North End in soccer?
14 What was the score?
15 Who scored two goals for West City?
16 What is the name of the new play by Hazel Margate?
17 When did it open?
18 Who saw the play?
19 Where did he stand after the play?
20 Who did he listen to?
21 Does he think the new play is good?
22 Does he think it's funny?
23 Does he think it's boring?
24 Is it going to rain tomorrow?
25 What will be dropping for the next few days?
26 Will the clouds clear up by tomorrow night?

Personal Questions

1 Do you listen to the radio often?
2 Which station or stations do you like?
3 Do you listen to the news on the radio or watch it on television?
4 Which news program do you like best?
5 What time is it on?
6 Do they give local, national, and world news?
7 How long does the news program last?
8 Do they give movie reviews?
9 Do they give the weather forecast?
10 In your opinion, is there too little, too much, or just enough news on radio and television?

In a radio studio

LESSON REVIEW

I Complete the sentences.

actor   bridge   review
awful   commuters   clear
audience   comedies   present
sports

1 You can cross the river now. The _____ is open.
2 Don't eat in that restaurant. The food is _____.
3 The _____ I like best are baseball and football.
4 The weather is bad now, but it will _____ up.

5   It's an excellent play. Everyone in the _____ liked it.
6   Some _____ take the train to the city. Others take the bus.
7   I like to laugh. That's why I like _____ best.
8   Robert was an _____ in plays and movies.
9   Please _____ these tickets at the door.
10 Will they _____ this movie for the newspaper?

II   Follow the model.

> Is Ellen studying now? →
> No, but she'll be studying in a few minutes.

1   Is Tom leaving for school now?
2   Is Miss Lyons working now?
3   Are the children eating now?
4   Is Edward swimming now?
5   Are you opening the store now?
6   Are the secretaries typing now?
7   Are you and Linda studying now?

III Change the words in italics to *by* and add the appropriate tag ending. Follow the model.

> The plane landed *not later than* three o'clock, _____? →
> The plane landed by three o'clock, didn't it?

1   The machine *near* the desk didn't work well, _____?
2   They got their pay *not later than* Friday, _____?
3   Mrs. Andrews didn't sit *near* you, _____?
4   Mr. and Mrs. Luke lived *near* the university, _____?
5   You stood *near* the entrance, _____?
6   I finished the report *not later than* noon, _____?
7   He didn't leave the machine *near* the door, _____?

IV   Rewrite the sentences. Change all nouns to pronouns. Follow the model.

> Mrs. Sanders gave the tickets to Mr. Drew. →
> She gave them to him.

1   Mr. Lewis gave the camera to his daughter.
2   The students saved the seat for the teacher.
3   I read the story to the children.
4   Miss Conlon sent the package to her brother.
5   Mrs. Shane bought the painting for me.
6   I made the statue for the Andersons.
7   She kicked the ball to you.

V   Write a local radio news report. Give a traffic report, sports news, weather forecast, and a movie review.

REGULAR VERBS _____

Infinitive	Present tense	Present participle	Past tense
1. to call	call, calls	calling	called
to play	play, plays	playing	played
to walk	walk, walks	walking	walked
to want	want, wants	wanting	wanted
2. to live	live, lives	living	lived
3. to hurry	hurry, hurries	hurrying	hurried
4. to stop	stop, stops	stopping	stopped
to plan	plan, plans	planning	planned

IRREGULAR VERBS _____

Infinitive	Present tense	Present participle	Past tense
to be	am, are, is	being	was, were
to become	become, becomes	becoming	became
to begin	begin, begins	beginning	began
to blow	blow, blows	blowing	blew
to bring	bring, brings	bringing	brought
to buy	buy, buys	buying	bought
to choose	choose, chooses	choosing	chose
to come	come, comes	coming	came
to cost	cost, costs	costing	cost
to eat	eat, eats	eating	ate
to fall	fall, falls	falling	fell
to feed	feed, feeds	feeding	fed
to feel	feel, feels	feeling	felt
to find	find, finds	finding	found
to fit	fit, fits	fitting	fit
to fly	fly, flies	flying	flew
to get	get, gets	getting	got
to give	give, gives	giving	gave
to go	go, goes	going	gone
to have	have, has	having	had
to hear	hear, hears	hearing	heard
to hurt	hurt, hurts	hurting	hurt
to know	know, knows	knowing	knew
to leave	leave, leaves	leaving	left
to let	let, lets	letting	let
to lose	lose, loses	losing	lost

Infinitive	Present tense	Present participle	Past tense
to make	make, makes	making	made
to meet	meet, meets	meeting	met
to pay	pay, pays	paying	paid
to read	read, reads	reading	read
to ride	ride, rides	riding	rode
to ring	ring, rings	ringing	rang
to run	run, runs	running	ran
to say	say, says	saying	said
to see	see, sees	seeing	seen
to sell	sell, sells	selling	sold
to send	send, sends	sending	sent
to set	set, sets	setting	set
to shoot	shoot, shoots	shooting	shot
to sit	sit, sits	sitting	sat
to sleep	sleep, sleeps	sleeping	slept
to speak	speak, speaks	speaking	spoke
to spend	spend, spends	spending	spent
to stand	stand, stands	standing	stood
to swim	swim, swims	swimming	swam
to take	take, takes	taking	took
to teach	teach, teaches	teaching	taught
to tell	tell, tells	telling	told
to think	think, thinks	thinking	thought
to understand	understand, understands	understanding	understood
to write	write, writes	writing	wrote

VOCABULARY

The number following each entry indicates the lesson in which the word was first presented.

a couple 5
a number of 4
actor 7
actress 7
advance 4
to afford 5
afraid 7
all 4
all over 3
ambition 6
animal 1
antenna 3
apartment 5
to approve 7
at first 3
audience 7
available 5
awful 7

to become 3
to blame 7
block 5
bookkeeping 6
bored 7
both 4
branch office 6
to breathe 1
bridge 7
brochure 4
busy 2

call 2
to call back 2
capital 5
care 4
career 6
channel 3
cheap 2
chemist 6
chemistry 6

choice 3
to clear up 7
close to 5
closed 7
closet 5
cloud 7
coin 2
comedy 7
common 6
commuter 7
complete 4
computer program-
  mer 6
to connect 2
connection 2
to cook 1
couple 5
cousin 1
cultural 3
cut 7

decision 5
to defeat 7
deposit 5
to dial 2
difference 2
difficult 6
direct 2
direct-dial 2
dirty 1
downtown 5

early 3
either 4
electricity 5
employer 6
employment
  agency 6
engaged 5
enormously 5

to enter 6
entertainment 3
entrance 7
even 4
event 3
excited 4
to exist 6
to expect 2
extra 2

fact 4
factory 3
far away 3
farm 1
to feed 1
field 6
finance 7
financial 6
former 6
free 2

gas 5
to get used to 5
to go on and on 6
to go sight-seeing 4

handsome 7
to hate 5
to have in mind 3
healthy 1
here 2
high 5
home 3
honeymoon 5
horse 1

in advance 4
in person 7